THE SECRET

OF MANIPULATION

The Techniques Of Persuasion And How To Analyze People Guide That Allows You To Take Mind Control.

implied. Readers acknowledge that the author is not engaging in the rendering of legal, financial, medical or professional advice. The content within this book has been derived from various sources. Please consult a licensed professional before attempting any techniques outlined in this book.

By reading this document, the reader agrees that under no circumstances is the author responsible for any losses, direct or indirect, which are incurred as a result of the use of information contained within this document, including, but not limited to, — errors, omissions, or inaccuracies.

TABLE OF CONNTENTS

INTRODUCTION

A manipulator is very good at talking about what's wrong and sowing doubt in the minds of others. He speaks only by generalities; he does not know how to listen and does not take responsibility for his words or actions. Finally, he preaches the false to know the true and prefers what is "foolish" to what is clear and simple.

Recognize the Type of Relationship He Has With Others

Whatever we do, it's never good enough. He knows or does better than others. He does not give any compliments, but always finds the small details that allow him to say that it is not perfect. The manipulator often destroys insidiously and cannot help but criticize. He would like to control everything, but since he can't do that, he shows his power by pointing out the weaknesses or mistakes of others. If we are proud of what we have accomplished, he will find a pretext for belittling us and devaluing us. When a parent adopts this type of behavior with his child (or a leader with his employee), he destroys the trust of his victim.

He Is Not Interested in Others

When the manipulator is concerned about any problem, his entire family must be in tune with his emotional state. Wife, husband, or children know that you have to become transparent so as not to attract anger. But everyone also knows that the manipulator always ends up finding a pretext to unload his fury. He's an ego crusher who knows everything better than everyone else. He always has an adventure, a story, or an anecdote more impressive than yours to make you think that you are small, lousy, or uninteresting.

He Is Surrounded By People Who Live in Fear and Failure

At work, with friends or family, we enjoy living in a pleasant atmosphere. Of course, there are times when there is conflict, screaming and arguing, but overall people know how to talk to each other. They trust each other and feel free to live and to do business.

When there is manipulation, the atmosphere is heavy

and people do not dare to speak to each other anymore. People isolate themselves in their suffering. Teachers know that when a child becomes isolated and self-contained, they are no longer involved in class and communicate with difficulty. This is a sign that something serious is happening (usually related to the abuse).

In the world of work, one can be certain of the presence of a manipulator from certain symptoms:

- People feel wrong

- The atmosphere is thick and heavy

- There is a lot of absenteeism and sick leave

- The new employees do not stay, and the old ones try to leave

- There are a lot of rumors and gossip

- People watch each other, are jealous of each other, and accuse each other

- People feel more or less strongly because of a lack of direction

- Decisions seem to be made on an ad hoc basis

- Promises are not kept

- Clans form and clash

- Work results drop or remain desperately low

- The staff is de-motivated and no longer believes in anything

- Projects rarely or hardly succeed

To impose his power and knowledge, the manipulator removes what works well and imposes complex and "silly things" that work poorly or which greatly disrupt the activity of all. He invests his energy in vain enterprises, and he frequently gives unjustified reproaches. He gives his opinion on everything and makes others doubt themselves by saying "nonsense" with the utmost confidence.

CHAPTER 1

WHAT IS MANIPULATIVE BEHAVIOR

The word manipulation is used primarily in our language with two senses, on the one hand, to refer in a general way to the handling that is carried out on various elements, utensils, which precisely require from those who employ them a finished knowledge and expertise. This is because they are objects that have in their functional structure an absolute consistency in the action they generate or perform when used.

And on the other hand, we use the term to designate that person or group, which using various characteristics that it has, such as the authority or power that it has in moral, social or political matters, uses it to get that person or group to not issue or express individual opinions, so that they do or not such or that thing.

That is, manipulation is what seeks to direct the opinion and thought of the other, nullifying their free will and their innate freedom, to orient it towards the end that best suits the manipulator.

On the political level and also in the contexts of mass media, manipulation, turns out to be a common currency that will have the purpose of getting the population or a sector to promote a political ideology or program, or to buy a particular product or service, among others.

It is worth mentioning that this conviction is carried out through a methodology in which the subtle prevails, and various effective persuasion techniques are put into practice , so that, of course, the recipient does not find a direct order or obligation to do something or think in such a way, but rather that the message in question decodes it as an opportunity or as the best alternative you can choose for something to be successful, among other options.

Although many strategies can be put into practice, among the most common are the appeal to emotions, the good ones, such as love, friendship, and also those that are feared, such as fear, or anguish.

And on the other hand, it is common to use the figure

of a person with authority in some aspect to exercise manipulation, mainly because that power that is recognized will be able to dominate or manage the opinions and actions that the manipulator wants to control.

CHAPTER 2

VICTIMS OF MANIPULATION

Just as predators have several traits they often all have, so to do their targets. The people that predators choose to target are typically chosen methodically, seeking out those who are least likely to rebel or try to fight back from any sort of manipulation. They can identify potential targets at a glance, needing little more than seconds to pass judgment on whether that person should be pursued with shocking accuracy. They can tell based off of body language, clothing, situations, interactions, and more, who will be able to serve them best, and they frequently act upon it. Here are some of the most common traits people who find themselves victims of manipulators often have.

Lacking Confidence

Due to lacking confidence, an individual can be quite easy to steamroll. Looking for body language that marks someone as lacking confident is a surefire way for predators to identify an easy target. Those who lack confidence are not likely to put up any sort of fight, either if you attack physically or emotionally. In lacking confidence, the predator can be sure that the individual also lacks the ability to defend boundaries or him or herself. When someone comes across as self-confident, he or she exudes an air of someone not as willing to put up with any sort of manipulation without a fight. Those with confidence will fight back when they feel wronged, violated, or hurt, and would have no qualms walking away from a relationship because they trust their own judgment.

By seeking someone lacking confidence, a predator goes after the easiest possible target to get whatever is desired, whether it is physical affection, arm candy, money, a home, a sale, a vote, or even just the feeling of having dominated someone else. The predator is able to boost his or her own ego through completely taking over another person's life and making decisions for the person. They may want someone around that will always defer to them, allowing them a position of power, even if it is undeserved or unwarranted. They may want someone to make them feel better about themselves, and someone with low self-confidence is likely to do that.

Sometimes, however, predators will go out of their way to identify someone with higher levels of confidence, as they see it as a game. They make it a challenge to so thoroughly break someone with high confidence that the target allows them to dominate the situation. This predator is doing nothing more than toying with the target and seeks nothing but self-gratification from doing so.

Have Something Desirable

Sometimes, personality has nothing to do with being targets. Sometimes, predators go after someone because they have something the predator wants. Whether it is money, status, a relationship, or anything else, the predator may choose to go after that person in hopes of getting it by association. If the person is someone powerful or influential, the predator may weasel her way into a friendship with the sole intention of pulling from that person's influence in the future. By winning what the other person perceives as a friendship, the manipulator creates an arsenal of people with a wide range of skills, abilities, and prestige that can be used when the need arises. If she wants a new job, she may be able to get a friend to pull strings and get her one, for example.

If what she desires is money, she may worm her way into a friendship or relationship with someone that has a lot of money in an attempt to attract that kind of lifestyle. If her boyfriend is wealthy, he would likely have little issue spending money on her. Further, she may feel as though associating herself with people who have what she wants will help her learn how to achieve what the other people have. Through learning what people are doing and how they are doing it, she may be able to emulate those behaviors in hopes of getting what she wants.

Caregiver-type

Some people are more prone to being caregivers than others. People who are compassionate can become easily manipulated because they seek to believe the best in others and seek to ensure that others' needs are met as thoroughly as possible. The caregiver-type person is likely to see the manipulator and all of his or her flaws, but proceed with a relationship anyway; believing that all that is needed to remedy the situation is love and patience. Unfortunately, that resilience to make sure that the manipulator is cared for and nurtured back to mental health also makes the caregiver an easy victim as well.

Because the caregiver is willing to take all of that negative behavior as signs that the manipulator needs more help, he or she will often completely overlook the warning signs and endure the manipulation, feeling as though it will stop eventually. Unfortunately, no amount of love or patience is going to change who someone is, and they are likely to be disappointed as the manipulative behaviors continue to grow, eventually beginning to drain on even the caregiver, whose personality type is prone to patience and resilience.

This is yet another common target for the manipulator because he or she can get away with far worse behavior far quicker than imagined. Because the manipulator knows that very little done will actually successfully push the caregiver away due to the caregiver's own inherent desire to fix the manipulator, the parasitic manipulator is able to continue to draw upon the caregiver's goodwill to get anything desired with few repercussions.

Empathetic

Considering that most of the manipulators you will encounter either lack empathy or know how to turn off their empathy to steel themselves from other people's emotional states, it should come as no surprise that they are naturally drawn toward the empathetic.

Empathy is the ability to sense and really understand how someone else is feeling. It is as if you have taken yourself and placed yourself in the other person's shoes, understanding exactly how they feel because you know how you would feel in their situation. This sense of putting yourself in someone else's shoes enables humans to ensure that those within their family or tribal unit are taken care of. It extends to other people as well, and those who are particularly empathetic find themselves identifying with other people. They may see the manipulator and decide that they see a person who is clearly in dire need of love and attention. They see the manipulator's flaws and want to try to fix them because they understand how lonely or down they would feel if they lacked confidence, lacked friends and family, or lacked whatever else it is that they believe the manipulator may be lacking.

The empathetic individual, like the caregiver, will take more than his or her fair share of abuse, justifying it as the manipulator being in a bad situation and that any rational person who had suffered the same way would behave similarly. The empathetic target is also far more susceptible to mind games relating to emotions and guilt trips, and the empathetic nature of the individual is eventually used as a weapon against him- or herself.

Dysfunctional Upbringing

People who have grown up in dysfunction have the disadvantage of never learning what normal, functioning, healthy relationships entail. They typically associate their own upbringing with what is normal and seek to replicate those sorts of relationships in adulthood. If a child grew up around parents who fought and argued all the time, with the mother always giving up what she wanted while the father took endlessly, the newfound adult is going to attempt to replicate that dynamic in any adult relationships.

Likewise, someone who grew up in dysfunction is not likely to understand how to set normal or healthy boundaries, or how to enforce those boundaries. They will be easily steamrolled, especially if boundaries being disrespected were a common theme growing up. This leaves the individual quite vulnerable, as he has no sense of normalcy and no sense of how to protect himself within a relationship. He does not understand that relationships are supposed to be symbiotic, and because of that, he is far more likely to deal with misbehaviors and abuse from a manipulator.

Knowing this, manipulators look for those who grew up in dysfunction. They are seen as easy targets. Their lack of boundaries make them easier to manipulate, and their lack of confidence or sense of what a healthy relationship looks like means that the target is not likely to see red flags when the manipulative behaviors begin cropping up. With red flags unseen, the manipulation is not seen as a warning sign that the relationship is unhealthy or should be ended. Particularly if abuse and manipulation were prevalent in childhood, the target may actually have a high tolerance for such behaviors, meaning the predator can escalate quickly and more effectively.

How to identify yourself as the Victim of Covert Manipulation

No one likes being manipulated. When manipulation occurs, you lose your power and your will. You must do what the other person wants. You often have no idea what the other person is really planning and you have no say in the situation. This makes life very difficult and it can cause you to do things that you don't want to do.

Now that you know the secrets to covert manipulation, you also know what to watch out for. You can reverse the techniques in this book to see when others are manipulating you. You can also flip these tactics on people and give them the manipulation that they are trying to run on you. There are various ways that you can protect yourself against manipulators.

Identify when You are a Victim

Everyone has a gut instinct that rears up when they are being used or misguided. Your gut instinct is very sound. You will know when you are a victim. The problem is, a lot of people ignore their instincts. You might ignore yours. You might think something like,

"I'm just being paranoid" or "What could possibly go wrong if I hang out with this person?" You might think that the harm will be worth the benefits that you could get from knowing this person who gives you bad vibes. Maybe everyone else likes this guy, so you think that you are just being weird and you should like him too. Or maybe he is able to charm you and convince you that he is not so bad and over time you start to get over your initial bad vibes.

But vibes are not something that you should ever ignore. The minute your gut warns you about someone, listen. Your first impression of someone is never wrong. If you get a bad first impression, don't give the person a second chance. You know more about someone by just glancing at them than you would think. The human brain is amazingly powerful; you only are conscious of roughly ten percent of your brain, so there is a lot going on under the surface that you are not consciously aware of. Your brain is capable of reading people and determining the future far more than you realize.

So when you get that gut feeling, understand that your brain is working very hard and noticing things that you are not consciously aware of. The person that you get bad vibes may not be matching his body language to his words, or he may be acting oddly in ways that you can't detect easily. Listen to your gut!

If you are just not in touch with your gut at all, or if you have doubts about someone, you might want to consider looking at some other signs. You can identify a manipulator based on his actions and language choices. You can also tell by how you feel around this person. There are various clues that point out who someone really is and what his intentions are.

What Makes You Vulnerable

You may wonder why manipulators are attracted to you, especially if you have had multiple encounters with manipulative types. You may also wonder what you should change about yourself to avoid running into a manipulator in the future.

One thing that makes you vulnerable is being accepting of manipulative treatment and emotional abuse. If you were emotionally abused or repressed as a child, this type of treatment may seem normal to you. You don't know anything else. You don't how a healthy relationship is supposed to feel. So you accept the terrible treatment that others would not think of accepting. As a result, you are projecting a sense of vulnerability that draws manipulators from far away. The minute you begin to tolerate their treatment and keep them in your life, they gain power over you and choose to keep using you until they get what they want. Work on increasing your self-esteem and avoiding familiar patterns. If you get that eerie sense of déjà vu when you meet someone, you might want to avoid that person because he is probably reminding you of previous abusive patterns that you have been in.

Another thing that may make you vulnerable is neediness or weakness. If you are in a vulnerable time in life, you might be more open to manipulators. Manipulators can see that you are in need and they see it as an opportunity to offer you what you need in exchange of what they really want. They will use any opportunity to gain control over you, and when you are in a bad period of life, you basically hand them opportunities. You need to guard your heart and mind especially well when you are at a disadvantage. Be wary of extremely kind strangers or life savers. Not all heroes are good guys. Your heroes may help you, but they may have hidden intentions. Most people won't do something for free so watch out.

You may also be a target for manipulation if you have low self-esteem. Events in your life or your childhood may have stripped away your self-esteem and confidence. You may be emotionally vulnerable. So you want people who build up your ego. Manipulators can spot this and they will move in on you, working hard to please you and make you smile. They see a way into your mind through your bruised ego. Try to build your self-esteem by yourself and work on loving yourself.

Signs of a Manipulator

A manipulator is often incredibly superficial. This means that he looks good on the outside, but there is nothing to follow it up on the inside. He is shallow and lacks depth. Everything he does and says is fake, part of a façade that he erects to fool you. So beware of people who are incredibly charming and attractive when you first meet them. Get to know them before you start confiding in them or trusting them. Don't make a commitment or business deal until you are absolutely sure of yourself.

Another sign of a manipulator is that you feel compelled to confide in him or to do what he wants. You constantly find yourself saying yes when you want to say no. It's impossible to be yourself and to stand up for yourself. He has some sort of power over you that you can't resist. Unfortunately, this power is just a carefully woven web of manipulation, deception, and emotional harm. He will dump you the minute he gets all that he can from you, so don't stick around or make the mistake of thinking that this relationship will last. He does not care, no matter how well he pretends to. Get away from him before the relationship gets too harmful and he ruins your life.

You may also find yourself saying sorry all of the time. Your guilt eats you up. Every situation with this person seems like your fault. Even if he is at fault, he manages to twist things around so that you feel guilty. He will never take responsibility for anything that he does and he will always put everything on you. He can do what he wants, but he holds you to exacting standards and punishes you when you don't follow suit. He basically kills your self-esteem and causes you to hate yourself.

Finally, a manipulator is great at changing your mind. You might feel one way, but after talking with him, you feel a completely different way. He is able to change your mind and your way of thinking. Sometimes this may even be a good thing, as he makes you think more constructively or positively. But be wary of someone who has so much power over your moods and your thoughts.

What Manipulation Feels Like

Often, in the early stages of a manipulative or emotionally abusive relationship, you will feel amazing. Your manipulator will be an expert at making you feel good about yourself. He will flatter you and fuel your ego.

Some people out there will make you feel good because they genuinely love you. But it often takes times for such a relationship to build. If someone whom you barely know is suddenly super into you and trying to rush a relationship, become very wary. Don't let things move too quickly. Get to know the person first. Someone who wants you so badly right off of the bat is usually superficial and just trying to prime you into a victim. Don't fall for it. Normal people don't just jump into relationships or try to rush things. Normal people also don't start acting crazy about you in an unusually short period of time.

A manipulator will make you feel like there are butterflies in your stomach. You will strive to please him. Your biggest desire will be to make him smile. This is because he is already making you feel as if you owe him or as if you like him so much that you will work to please him. Beware of people who make you feel like a puppet. You should never want to bend over backwards for someone so urgently. You need to have a sense of dignity and personal space and value in every relationship. If you don't, something is off.

You will also feel guilty about the smallest things. You may feel inadequate or guilty for not always pleasing this person every day. A sense of guilt about living or being you may haunt you. You may feel ashamed of who you are. These feelings may seem to come out of the blue, but this is just because you are with a super covert manipulator. Trust me, he is playing some serious games with your heart to inspire your guilt. These feelings are not random or spontaneous, but rather part of your manipulator's carefully crafted plan to hurt you. So you should become suspicious and understand that these feelings are not a normal element of a healthy relationship.

Your self-esteem will certainly dive when you spend time around a manipulator. Soon, your confidence will become riddled with holes. You will be poisoned with self-doubt and angst. This is not a good thing and you should not stay around someone who does this to you.

You also will probably start to feel crazy. You will wonder if you have an undiagnosed disorder or if you are falling apart at the seams. When you argue with this person, he will deny everything that he just said. He will call you nuts for arguing with him or claim that you are just making things up. In addition, he will invent elaborate stories and blame you for things that you never did, often so convincingly that you start to believe that you did what he claims. He will also challenge your perception of reality, lie through his teeth, and make you question yourself constantly. All of these things combined will tear at your self-esteem and consciousness, making you question your sanity. Manipulators can actually rewire the neurons of your brain and do permanent damage to your mental health and personality, so you should not stick around.

One great piece of advice is that if you feel the need to record someone during arguments because he denies what he says later and makes you feel crazy, then you are in an emotionally abusive relationship and you should leave now. You are not crazy. This person is just gaslighting you.

What to Do when Someone is Manipulating You

The simplest piece of advice on how to deal with a manipulator is to just up and leave. If you can do this, great. You should immediately. There will be no good to come from this relationship, so why stay around and get hurt?

But this advice is often easier said than done. There are some situations where you cannot escape a manipulator and his traps. For instance, you might have to work with a manipulator and you can't just quit your job, or you don't want to. Or you might have a manipulative family member and you can't cut him off or you will lose all of your family. You may feel trapped and unable to leave for various reasons, such as financial reasons. Maybe you have kids with the manipulator and must speak to him or her for the rest of your life regarding the children. Co-parenting doesn't automatically end when your children turn eighteen; sometimes, you have to continue a relationship with the father or mother well into your children's' adult lives, and you must be around each other for your children's weddings, graduations, grandchildren, etc. Or maybe there is a manipulative friend in your group whom everyone else likes. There are countless reasons why you may be stuck with a manipulator in your life. Leaving is not always a viable option.

Having a Manipulative Partner and How to Avoid Manipulation

What is a Narcissistic Personality?

The word 'narcissist' comes from a story in Greek mythology, where Narcissus fell in love with his own image. The narcissistic personality is defined as a person who idealized their own self-image and attributes to the point of negatively affecting other people's lives. Many people possess narcissistic traits when it has to do with a certain section of their lives, but also possess a healthy dose of humility and self-doubt. This is not the case for a person with a narcissistic personality.

In 2004, psychiatrists Hotchkiss and James F. Masterson listed what they called the Seven Deadly Sins of Narcissism:

Lack of /bad boundaries: Boundaries simply do not exist for a person who is a full-blown narcissist. They are unaware that other people can exist not solely to suit their needs, and that other people may have different thoughts or feelings than themselves. Narcissistic supply is a term used to describe how narcissist relies on codependents in order to fill their sense of self-worth.

Exploitation: The narcissist may employ exploitation without regard for the feelings of others. This is usually done to another person who is in a position of subservience and cannot escape it, such as in a work setting or children at school.

Entitlement: Believing that they are special and deserve special treatment and begin expressing narcissistic rage they are denied it (a reaction when a threat to their self-worth is perceived).

Arrogance: A narcissist likes to raise their own self-importance by degrading others.

Envy: A narcissist may employ the feeling of contempt toward another person in order to avoid feelings of jealousy in reaction to the result of another person's achievements.

Magical Thinking: A psychological defense mechanism that allows them to see themselves as flawless and project shame onto others rather than feel it themselves.

Shamelessness: Narcissists do not express feeling shame for any behavior or belief they may possess, as the sensation of feeling shame implies that they must have done something wrong.

Narcissistic Personality Disorder (NPD)

NPD is a personality disorder that expresses a long-term pattern of behavior that is self-focused, superior, and exploitative of others and severely lacks empathy for others. The difference between NPD and the previously described traits of a person with a narcissistic personality is the consistency of the traits and to what extent they impair their lives. This difference is described as pathological; when the expression of these traits consistently disrupts the lives of the narcissist, it is when a mental health diagnosis is given. Many people possess narcissistic personality traits and are able to live a successful and stress-free life, while those with NPD may perceive themselves this way, are actually not developing and achieving success due to the crippling fear of criticism, self-doubt, and failure that lies under their inflated sense of self-worth.

The Malignant Narcissist

These kinds of narcissists are ones that are not bothered by guilt and has the ability to resemble antisocial personality disorder. APD is another personality disorder defined primarily by antisocial behavior that has no consideration for right and wrong. The malignant narcissist may take pleasure in causing pain and display forms of sadistic behavior. The key difference though between a malignant narcissist and an antisocial personality is the way the person relates to others. Narcissists share a codependent relationship with others, and deep down, require the approval of others in order to function. A person with antisocial personality disorder could not care less about the opinion of others and do not require the engagement of other people in order to feel validated.

The Narcissist and Emotional/Psychological Abuse: What Truly Lies Beneath

Abuse is the behavioral act that a narcissist applies as a defense mechanism against a variety of emotions that the narcissist is constantly attempting to suppress. Despite the outward expression of self-importance, grandiosity, lacking empathy, and cruel behavior, the narcissist is actually acting out of deeply repressed sensations of fear. They fear rejection, their own imperfections and shortcomings, of being abandoned, unwanted, and unloved.

The following section will summarize 14 behavioral expressions of a narcissist and how it connects to being abusive. A narcissist could be an authority figure, a parent, a partner, a teacher, a coach, or a caregiver. Marjalis Fjelstad writes about the behaviors to look out for if you believe someone in your life is a narcissist on Mind Body Green.

Narcissists feel the need to be the best/most at everything in their lives. Even if it means the sickest or injured, they must be at the top.

A narcissist constantly feels the need to acquire validation from a partner or important person in their lives because they subconsciously believed that they are not good enough. External validation is always required, but never enough. They will always want you to praise them because they cannot provide the confidence and assurance for themselves, despite the outward appearance of confidence and egotism.

Narcissists are perfectionists, which means that those in their lives must be perfect, they must be perfect, and everything that they have planned or envisioned for themselves must play out without a hitch. This, of course, is not how life works, which often leads to the narcissist feeling dissatisfied. Perfectionism is why it is endlessly difficult for a narcissist to receive any criticism, even if it is constructive.

Because of the perfectionism, narcissist wants to control everything around them, and this includes a partner, a child, a parent, etc. This is where control in abusive relationships comes from; because the behavior of the victim is not lining up with the exact ways the abuser wants it to.

Narcissists never take responsibility for their actions. Even if they contributed to the not so flawless way something may have been carried about, the fault is never their own. It is yours because you did do exactly as you were instructed. Nothing they ever do can be wrong.

As previously stated, a narcissist cannot comprehend what boundaries are. They cannot comprehend that you have your own thoughts, feelings, expectations, and past. They do not like when another person expresses feelings that oppose their own, because it is not perfect, which leads to more behaviors that attempt to control their entire world.

The narcissist lacks empathy, which is why they are unable to understand boundaries. They cannot correctly read body language or facial expressions because they believe that other people must feel the same way they do. However, they are also overly sensitive and aware of perceived rejection from others, and constantly believe that the source of their negative feelings is caused by the person they are closest to in their life.

Logic does not work with the narcissist. Trying to explain to a narcissist how their behavior affects you is futile because they are only aware of their own thoughts and feelings.

Splitting is a term used to describe how narcissists categorize every feeling, person, and experience into one of two categories: the good and the bad. This is due to their intense sense of perfectionism. Nothing can be a combination of a positive valence experience and a negatively perceived one. They can only cope with the single experience that is their own.

An appearance of surety and self-confidence hide the true narcissist experience of fear; fear of failure, losing money, their partner leaving them, their children being taken away, etc. No matter how close a person can get to a narcissist, they will never be able to build a trusting relationship, simply because the narcissist is in constant fear of being abandoned.

Anxiety is a looming sensation for the narcissist, who projects this sensation onto their siblings, partner, or parent. This is not an enjoyable sensation for the narcissist, so they rather throw it onto someone else.

Shamelessness may appear to be a trait of the narcissist, but it is truly an expression of the opposite. Shame means that there is something wrong about a person, and the narcissist cannot cope with this notion. Feeling shame is the enemy, so they do not allow themselves to feel it and bury it deep inside their subconscious. They hate that they possess insecurities and fear, and live with this lingering sensation that becomes projected on the closest loved one who may 'find them out.'

Since the narcissist doesn't want to accept that they feel fear or insecurities, they are unable to feel vulnerable. This makes it difficult to create and maintain close intimate relationships. The narcissist is constantly displaying this flawless sense of self-importance and perfection to the point where the true human beneath that is hidden from those that the narcissist considers the most important.

Lack of empathy means that the narcissist cannot work or communicate in a group setting, because only their wants, needs, and thoughts are what truly exists in their world.

CHAPTER 3

HOW TO USE DARK PSYCHOLOGY TO MANIPULATE OTHERS

Dark psychology is an art and a science—it seeks to manipulate others in a way that controls the other person. Through a series of behaviors such as manipulation, coercion, or persuasion, an individual seeks to get exactly what he or she wants, no matter the cost. By and large, people care about how other people feel, and endeavor to behave ethically and acceptably, but what about the minority of people who do not?

What is Dark Psychology?

Dark psychology refers to the mindset and techniques people can use to get what they want. Often aligned with the dark triad and manipulative people seeking to better themselves while harming everyone around them, dark psychology can be an effective skill to develop and master for yourself if you have to interact with other people. In fact, many people in public positions or positions of power turn to dark psychology to learn how to better get the results they want. Even salespeople frequently are taught skills that would fall within the list of dark psychology manipulation or mind control.

Keep in mind that there is manipulation, and there is an influence. Influence is normal; it involves swaying others to allow for goals to be worked toward. When influencing others, boundaries are honored and it is based on honest communication and respect for the other person, including respecting if the other person decides not to do whatever it is you would like. In contrast, manipulation is covert and coercive. The manipulator uses cunning and power to sway the other person. Rather than communicating clearly, the manipulator may lie or over-exaggerate in order to get the desired result. They may assert that they are in a position of power that they may or may not have, and they will push you to oblige them, preying on anything they can in order to get what they want. People are expendable. People's values are expendable. Anything is expendable if it means their desires are met.

Dark psychology's manipulation is primarily selfish. Every bit of manipulation is to ensure that the individual's wants come to exist. They do not care about the outcomes, or how it may impact the other person—they are only concerned with themselves.

These sorts of manipulative tactics and tendencies are encountered on a daily basis in a wide range of situations. Even television ads may inundate you with attempts to sway your perceptions of things in hopes of getting you to buy their products. In a world filled with constant attempts to manipulate you and sway your thoughts, you may be thinking, how can you possibly understand how to protect yourself from it? Or even better, how can you begin tapping into those skills to use them ethically to see the results you hope to achieve? The first step to this understands the key facets of dark psychology, from how it works to why people use it. Understanding and learning this information will prepare you understanding why.

How Dark Psychology Works

The entire construct of dark psychology and manipulation may seem difficult to understand—after all, avoiding falling for manipulation seems like an easy enough tasks to have, right? Unfortunately, manipulation can be quite covert, hiding underneath a thin veil of deniability and other pretty wrappings designed to keep the insidious nature of the manipulation undetected. There are several theories for how manipulation may go undetected, but for the purposes of this book, we will use one.

According to the psychologist, George K. Simon, there are three key aspects that make manipulation successful. These are:

Hiding the true intentions and behaviors behind something more friendly or good-natured. The truth may be hidden behind faux concern or authority.

Understanding the target's vulnerabilities so you can deliberately choose how to proceed. The manipulator takes the time to understand anything that can be exploited.

Being callous enough to not feel guilty at inflicting harm to the target if doing so becomes necessary. Even if whatever is done causes physical, mental, financial, or other harm, that is acceptable. Ultimately, the only person who matters is the manipulator, and the only goals that matter are his or her own.

Attempts at coercion and manipulation meet these three standards to be sufficiently successful to work. For example, imagine that you sell cars and you want to convince someone to buy a car that will land you a better commission. You would go through these three steps to influence your customer into buying them. First, you would likely want to disguise your interest in selling someone a specific car as concern for them. If they want to buy an older car, you may try to upsell the safety features of the newer model in hopes of convincing them to buy the more expensive car, or you may show how this newer model has some new feature that you exaggerate to make sound imperative to them. If they have children, you may try to emphasize how the trunk can be opened hands-free, or that there are a backup camera and sensors in the bumpers that will alert them in case a child were to sneak behind them.

Knowing that the parents are likely to be easily swayed by appeals to emotion, you may offhandedly mention how you had heard a story in the news about someone who accidentally ran over their child backing up, and that it was too bad that their car had not been equipped with the backup camera. You use your knowledge that parents are typically quite vulnerable when it comes to the welfare of their children and use that knowledge to your advantage.

Because you are detached from the target and motivated to sell, you do not feel any guilt about telling them the story. You want to instill fear in them that makes them feel like spending more money is necessary for the protection of their child's life. You want them to fear the consequences that could potentially follow if they do not do what you want. You want them to feel like their only option is to follow through with buying the car.

Ultimately, the three of those criteria combine, and you end up with the intended effect—the parents agree to buy a car out of their original price range out of fear of running over their child. You successfully took advantage of the situation, reading the situation and understanding exactly how best to proceed. These are the fundamentals of beginning to manipulate others.

No one enjoys being taken for a ride; no one likes

being played for a fool either. Unfortunately, many people have these unpleasant experiences in almost every facet of human interaction. Worst of all, it happens to a lot of us more than once! The intriguing thing is not that we were played for fools; rather, it is that we come out of the experience with a determination to never fall for such tricks ever again only to find that we have been tricked again and again.

Perhaps, this book you are reading right now is the wakeup call you need to jar you out of your psychological slumber and do something practical about your decision to not have a repeat experience of emotional manipulation ever again.

What is Emotional Manipulation?

For the sake of clarity, let us have a working definition of what emotional manipulation is.

Emotional manipulation is the temporal takeover of your ability to think and act rationally. When someone acts or says things that distract or bypasses your rational and conscious mind, and then hijacks your emotions to the point of influencing you to feel a certain way or behave in a certain way, they are, at that moment, manipulating your emotions.

Such people who have practiced the art of emotional manipulation or who have developed the bad habit of manipulating others are capable of making you do what you would normally not do. Beyond making you behave in negative ways, shrewd influencers can completely ruin your career, destroy your love life, and cause havoc in your relationship with others. It doesn't matter how academically intelligent you are, if you do not take steps to protect yourself from emotional saboteurs by developing your emotional intelligence, you may learn the hard way why being street smart is as equally important as being book smart.

Emotional manipulation is simply a mind game. Although some people have psychopathic and sociopathic issues, while others go through some training to attain mastery in the art of mind games, everyone is born with the ability to manipulate others for positive and for negative purposes. Children do not need formal training in neuro-linguistic programming before they can push their parents' guilt buttons, neither do they have to be coached before they use flattery to warm their way into the hearts of parents and adults right before they present their requests. Passive aggression doesn't have to be taught to any child before they use it to manipulate parents and adults into submission. These things are inborn and can be used for the benefit of all involved in any interaction (a win-win situation) or strictly for the selfish benefit of the manipulator.

Usually, those who are manipulated emotionally have unknowingly surrendered a part of their self-esteem, self-worth, and self-image to the manipulator. This is why the longer a victim stays in a manipulative relationship (either personal or professional relationship), the more damage is done to their overall sense of self.

As you will discover from reading this book, self-awareness is a very important quality to develop if you must accomplish your goal of not falling again for manipulators. The more aware you are of your emotions and your tendency to react to others, the greater your chances of gaining control of your thoughts, emotions, and your behavioral response.

Look at it from this angle: since emotional manipulation is all about mind games, the person with greater control of your emotions wins the game. So, if you gain control over your thoughts, emotions, and behaviors, there is little to no chance that you will be played for a fool again and again.

Let us now give our attention to finding out who a manipulator is, their goals, and the tools with which they use in the art of manipulation.

Who is a Manipulator?

In the simplest terms, a manipulator is someone who uses people to influence the outcome of a situation usually to their benefit. In other words, when someone gets you to think and act in ways that please them, they have manipulated you. The outcome that a manipulator seeks can include:

To use their victim to gain access to power or to seize power.

To gain partial or total control in a relationship or at work.

To take the credit for another person's hard work.

To enjoy the benefits of their victim's hard work.

To make another person take the fall for their faults.

To achieve their devious goals, manipulators can use any of the following tools:

- Deceit – deliberately withholding vital information, misleading with words, actions, or inactions, being dishonest, and being generally fraudulent.

- Guilt – making you feel responsible for an unfortunate outcome.

- Lies – deliberately twisting the truth or spreading outright falsehood about their victims.

- False hope – making empty promises, using future events that may not ever occur as baits for their victims.

An emotional manipulator has a deep-seated need to be in control. Underneath that desire to always be in control of people and situations is the feeling of insecurity. To mask that insecurity, an emotional manipulator will sometimes put on the appearance of someone domineering and powerful.

A person who is in the habit of manipulating others has

little to no regard about how his or her behavior affects their victims or others around them. Their desire to be in control and to feel superior is more important to them than any other thing. This is why they carefully seek out vulnerable individuals who will dance to their tune and validate them. When you succumb to a manipulator or even react in an emotional outburst, you give them power over you.

Why People are Emotionally Manipulated

From ill-famed world leaders to leaders in the workplace and other social settings, emotional manipulation has been used to rally followers around selfish causes or goals. Emotionally charged speeches, well-timed body gestures, sarcasm, intimidation, aggression, and false hope have been used to get people to stop thinking and just act blindly! The question is: why do people tend to easily fall for these types of mind control tactics?

I am not implying that only people under another person's authority can be negatively influenced. In reality, your station in life doesn't matter much when it comes to emotional manipulation. You could be a follower, subject, sibling, child, subordinate, student, or any other person and still be able to negatively influence your superior. Isn't this why kids have their way with parents? Have you not witnessed or heard of bosses who are incapable of asserting their official powers over a particular employee because that employee has them wrapped around his or her fingers?

Why then do people of all class and position fall for manipulators? Two reasons stand out from all the other possible reasons: unhealthy self-esteem and fear. A person with healthy self-esteem does not need flattery to recognize their self-worth, neither does he or she respond to covert and overt aggression. Since they recognize the inherent and inalienable worth of every person, it is difficult to get them distracted by a feeling of pity for anybody. Having healthy self-esteem ensures that you are not easily pushed into feeling guilty for someone else's actions or inactions.

However, unhealthy self-esteem can make an individual seek validation of their self-worth from external sources. When a manipulator gets wind of this fact, he preys on that weakness by temporarily soothing their emotional need. As soon as the victim becomes comfortable and lets down their emotional guard, the manipulator nudges, and sometimes, coerces them into doing things they would not have normally done.

Fear, on the other hand, drives people to succumb to a manipulator even long after they have discovered that the person is using them. Fear is the reason why a lot of people remain in a manipulative, controlling and toxic relationship. They fear:

Loss of basic needs: for those who are in a relationship where their daily sustenance depends 100% on a manipulative partner, they may continue to endure such emotional control tactics because of the fear of losing their only means of survival.

Confrontation: many people would rather avoid arguments and conflicts that are likely to arise from being firm and courageous. Confrontation gives them the jitters.

Discomfort: this refers to doing everything possible to stay clear of the awkward feeling that being assertive can bring about. Some people prefer the seeming peace than the uneasiness that will result in their relationship if they were to take steps to protect themselves from being controlled emotionally.

Loss of friendship or partnership: some people go to great lengths to keep their relationship even when it is causing them deep hurts and subjecting them to negative influences. They simply cannot picture themselves without the other person; they are loyal to a fault. This makes them open to all sorts of manipulation as the other person takes undue advantage of their loyalty.

Loss of opportunity: this refers to remaining compliant and submissive to gain or keep an opportunity like free accommodation, gainful employment, and other benefits.

It is important to note that emotional control may not always present as someone trying to dominate and oppress you, at least, not at first. In many cases, it presents as being pleasant and nice but it later turns into manipulation and control.

If you are in a relationship that has any of the above characteristics, then you are in an emotionally controlling relationship. It is doing a lot of damage to your self-esteem. Over a long time, you will feel worthless and completely dependent on the other person.

There is a need to free yourself from such manipulation if you must regain your self-esteem. Thankfully, this is the focus of the rest of this book.

Manipulation Techniques

Mastering the art of mental manipulation can be rewarding. Remember that a manipulator is going to try as much as they can to reach their end goal. To attain this end goal, the manipulator will apply any technique that they can to make people do what they want. The conventional techniques that manipulators like to use to fulfill their end goals include:

Blackmail

Emotional blackmail

Lying

Putting down the other person

Creating an illusion

These are going to be discussed in detail plus many different techniques not listed here.

However, if you are planning to use them, you need to be smart, practice a lot, and soon you can change the way others think and behave.

Let us dive in and discuss all the techniques in details. Are you ready?

In the moral debate, manipulating minds of other people may appear unethical for many-and for a good reason. Basically, you are playing with other people's feelings, thoughts, and emotions for your own good. But it is up to you to decide what is right and what is not. This chapter guides you on methods that manipulators use to influence others.

You can attain a lot of emotional and financial advantage if you master how to play your cards right an how to make other people do whatever you want them to do whether men or women. The secret is to do it in such a way that they don't discover they are being manipulated. Don't forget the basic requirements that manipulators must fulfill for them to succeed.

Blackmail

Blackmail is the first method that manipulators may

apply. Blackmail is described as an act that that involves threats that are unjustified to achieve a specific gain or trigger a loss to the subject unless the manipulator's demand is realized. It can also be described as an act of coercion that encompasses threats of prosecution as criminal, dangers of grabbing the target's property or money, or even risks of causing physical pain to the subject. There is a long history of blackmail. Initially, it was a phrase that referred to a payment that the settlers left to the area that was neighboring Scotland to the chieftains in charge. This payment was made to provide the settlers with security from the marauders and thieves that were moving to England. Since then, it has changed to mean something different, and in some cases, it is an offense in the US. For the sake of this section, blackmail is more than sending threats, either emotional or physical, to the subject to coerce them into performing what the manipulator requires.

In some cases, blackmail is described as a form of extortion. While there are occasions when the two are used interchangeably, there are some slight differences. For instance, extortion occurs when someone grabs the personal property of another by threatening to harm the person if the property is not given. On the flipside, blackmail happens when threats are applied to prevent the subject from taking part in lawful activities. Sometimes, these two events may work together. The individual may threaten someone and demand money to be set at bay and not harm the subject.

The manipulator is going to use this technique to achieve what they want. They are going to spend time to learn a thing of personal nature concerning their subject and then use that as a means of blackmail against them. They may blackmail their subject by threatening to send an embarrassing secret or even by destroying their opportunities of landing a new job or promotion. Or the manipulator might operate more shockingly by threatening to physically harm their subject or the family of the subject if they fail to agree with the manipulator. Whatever the blackmail may be, it is used to assist the manipulator in reaching the final goal with the help of the subject.

Emotional blackmail

It is another tactic that can be used by the manipulator. In the following technique, the manipulator will aim to inspire sympathy or guilt in their subject. These two emotions the strongest for humans to feel and they will always be sufficient to trigger the subject into the action that the manipulator requires. The manipulator is going to take advantage of this to achieve what they want. They will apply the sympathy or guilt that they motivate to coerce the subject into cooperating. The level of sympathy or guilt will always be blown out of proportion, causing the subject to likely help in the situation.

The reason for using this technique is to play around with the emotions of the subject. In the normal blackmail, the subject has to deal with a threat, mainly in terms of physical harm to themselves or a person they love. For emotional blackmail, the manipulator will attempt to activate emotions that are strong enough to incite the subject to act.

Although the subject may feel like they are helping out of their free will, the manipulator has worked to make sure that the subject is helping and will and will trigger the emotions again when it is required.

Putting down the other person

There are many alternatives manipulators have when they want to make their subject to help them attain their end goal. One successful approach is when the manipulator can put down their subject. In normal situations, if the manipulator applies verbal skills to put their subject down, they will run a high risk of causing the subject feel like a personal attack has been put on them. When the subject feels like they have been attacked, they will bristle and avoid helping the manipulator in a way that they would like. However, the subject will not like the manipulator and will distance from the manipulator as far as they can, making it difficult for the manipulator to realize their end goal.

This is the reason why the manipulator is not going to move around and put down their target. They need to be discreet about the process and look for a way to do it without making the subject feel like they are being attacked. One way that this can be accomplished is through humor. Humor can reduce the barriers that may otherwise appear because humor is funny and makes people happy. The manipulator can change their insult into a joke. While the put down has been converted into a joke, it will work effectively as if the joke was not present without creating any scars on the subject.

Usually, the manipulator will instruct their subject in the form of a third person. This allows them to mast whatever they are saying quickly plus offering an easy means to deny causing harm if it comes back to haunt them later on.

For instance, they may begin their put down with "other people" if the subject can guess that the comments were made at them, then the manipulator would finish it with a throwaway line that may include something like "present company excepted, of course."

The concept of the put down is to make the subject feel like they are less than the manipulator. It upgrades the manipulator to a new level and leaves the subject feeling like something is needed. The subject is likely to improve things and correct any wrong that they have made. This will make the manipulator powerful, and they will easily get the subject to help them.

Lying

Regardless of the manipulator's end goal, lying is a tactic that they are an expert in and which they will exercise all the time to get what they want. A manipulator can use different forms of lies to allow them to realize their end goal. One is that they can lie entirely and in some cases, eliminate elements of truth from their subjects.

When a manipulator tells a lie, it is because they are aware that the lie is going to progress their agenda more effectively than the truth. Telling someone the fact may cause them not to want to assist the manipulator and that would go against their plans.

Instead, the manipulator will lie to get the target convinced to do something for them and by the time the subject discovers the lie, it is too late to correct the issue.

The manipulator may choose to remove part of the truth in the stories they narrate. In this approach, they are going to say parts of the truth but will hide certain things that prevent the progress made. These lies can be dangerous because it will become increasingly challenging to tell the reality of the story and what the lie is.

It is critical to note that when you are working with the manipulator, anything that they tell you could be a lie. It is not a great idea to trust anything that the manipulator is saying because they are attempting to abuse and use their subjects to reach the end goal. The manipulator is going to do and say anything possible, even lying to achieve what they want, and they aren't going to feel sorry about it. As long as they accomplish what they want, they are not too concerned about how it is changing the subject or others close to them.

Building an illusion

Apart from lying, the manipulator is going to be an expert at creating illusions that are capable of generating their final goal more effectively. They will work to build a picture that they want and then convince the target that this illusion is a reality; whether or not it doesn't matter to the manipulator. To achieve this, the manipulator is going to generate the evidence that is required to prove the point that works to their purpose.

To begin the illusion, the manipulator has to plant the ideas and evidence into the minds of the target. Once the intentions are in place, the manipulator will step back for some days and allow the manipulation to happen in the minds of the subjects over that period.

After that period, the manipulator will have an opportunity to get the subject to follow the plan.

Manipulation is a method of mind control that is hard for the subject to avoid. Manipulation can happen in daily life, and in some cases, it can happen without the subject having enough power of it. The manipulator is going to work discreetly to attain their end goal without getting the target suspicious and affect the process. The manipulator will not worry about who they are harming or how others may feel, and most of them are not capable of mastering the needs of their subjects.

They know that they need something and that the subject they have selected is going to assist them in achieving their goal.

The strategies that are explored in this chapter are designed to help describe what happens during the manipulation process and how the brain of the manipulator operates. It is always good to distance from someone who may be a manipulator so that you can avoid this form of mind control.

The fear and relief technique

In a nutshell, the fear-and-relief method requires a person to play with the other person's emotions. Although this technique can indeed generate a lot of stress and anxiety, it is very effective.

The method has two parts: First, make the other person fear something. It will rapidly make him vulnerable to the illogical behavior that you can apply for your advantage. Then you can provide him with a relief of the fear that he experiences. The most challenging part of this technique is to determine what to use to scare another person. Of course, you cannot continue to come up with scary things hoping that the other person will begin to be scared. You need to be creative and come up with a smart idea of what you are going to say and how you are going to say before you approach the person. Then you need to be armed with a solution that will save him from the uncomfortable feeling.

The technique is always applied in the media to catch the attention of viewers. For instance, the news channel can scare people with a dramatic headline. Then they end up with what you need to do, "keep watching for the updated information of what to do."

Probably, you know that you are not a news channel, but that doesn't imply that you cannot use fear and relief method to manipulate others. You can scare people with anything ranging from their career goals to personal relationships. Be creative, study your target and develop the best strategies of doing the method.

Once you realize that the person you want to manipulate is going to give up, that is when you assist them in relieving stress and releasing all the steam. You are attempting to give that person mood swings that will make him or her completely disarmed. When that occurs, the person in question is more likely to perform whatever you need them to, as evil as that may appear.

CHAPTER 4

MANIPULATION TECHNIQUES

Everyone in the world has likely used manipulation at some points in their lives. This could have been through telling the most straightforward lies to get out of situations or by flirting with others to get what you want. In understanding the techniques used by manipulators in their work, you need to ask yourself the following question:

Who is at threat from a manipulator? To regulate their victims, the pullers of the strings (manipulators) use several tactics, but most importantly, they do this by targeting specific kinds of personalities. You are more likely to be a victim of manipulation if you have low self- esteem, if you are inexperienced, pleased easily, if you are not confident about yourself and if you lack assertive instincts.

What are the requirements for successful manipulation? Primarily, successful manipulation encompasses a manipulator. Manipulation is also likely to be achieved through covert hostile methods. For successful persuasion, a manipulator has to:

- Cover their violent purposes, deeds, and be friendly.

- Be aware of the psychological susceptibilities of the targeted person so as to conclude which strategies are likely to be the most effective.

- Have an adequate level of callousness to have no doubts about triggering injury to the victim if necessary.

- The manipulators exploit different defenselessness habits that exist in the victim's character and such include:

- The naïveté of the targeted person - Based on naïveté, the targeted person experiences hardships to buy the notion that many human beings are always sneaky, deceitful, and hard-nosed. This means if you are the victim, you will be in denial that you are being victimized.

- If you are over-conscientiousness - This is where you find yourself ready to grant the exploiter the advantage of distrust. The manipulator ends up blaming you and supporting their side, which makes you trust them easily. If you are too honest, you end up thinking everyone else is reliable as well.

- Self-confidence - Controllers often check whether you are a self-doubting person and whether you lack self-assertiveness, and this makes you go into a defensive mode effortlessly. You end up not giving a second thought about errors.

- Over-intellectualization - This makes it hard for you to understand and therefore, you end up believing your manipulator's reasons for being hurtful.

- Your emotional reliance - If you have a submissive personality, you are more likely to be a victim of manipulation. The more you rely on your emotions, the more vulnerable you are to being manipulated.

- Loneliness - If you are a lonely person, you are likely to agree to take little proposals of social interaction. Some manipulators will propose being your companion, but at a price. This also involves being narcissistic whereby, you fall easily for any kind of unjustified flattery. Lonely people act without any consultations. Therefore, loneliness goes hand in hand with being impulsive.

- Materialistic - Having a get-rich-quick mindset makes you cheap prey for manipulators. This means you are greedy and want to get rich quickly, hence end up acting immorally for some sort of material exchange.

- The elderly are also at a higher risk of getting controlled easily because they are fatigued and not able to multitask. Likelihoods the elderly will have a thought that a manipulator might be a conman are very rare. Manipulators thus take advantage of them and commit elder abuse.

Techniques of Manipulation

Manipulators take time to explore and examine your characteristics and find out how vulnerable you are to exploitation. They tend to control their victims by playing with their psychological characters. Having read the points above, now you need to know what the tactics and techniques are manipulators use to control their victims. They include various methods, as discussed below.

Techniques of manipulation

Reinforcement: This can be either positive, negative, or intermittent forms of reinforcement.

- Positive reinforcement: This involves the case where the manipulator uses praises, charms, crocodile tears, unnecessary apologizing, public acknowledgment, cash, presents, consideration, and facial languages like forced laughter or smiles.

- Negative reinforcement: A manipulator removes you from a negative situation as a favor.

- Intermittent reinforcement: This is also known as partial reinforcement. This creates an environment full of fear and doubts. It encourages the victim of manipulation to persist.

Punishment: The manipulator acts in a nagging manner. There is yelling, silent treatment, intimidating behavior, and threatening of the victim. Manipulators cry and tend to play the victim card, thus emotionally blackmailing the victim and can go further by swearing they are the innocent one.

Lying: it entails two ways; lying by commission and lying by omission.

1. Lying by commission - You will find it hard to tell when a manipulator is lying the moment they do it, and the truth won't reveal itself until it is too late. You should understand that some people are experts at lying and thus you should not give in easily to their tactics.

2. Lying by omission - This is a subtle way used to manipulate, and it entails telling lies, and at the same time, withholding significant amounts of the facts. It is also applied in propaganda.

Denial: Manipulators rarely admit they are wrong. Even when they have done something wrong, they will refuse to believe it. They are rational and always assert that their behavior is not harmful or they are not as bad as someone else has explained. They accompany every exploitation with phrases like, 'it was only a joke'.

Attention: This includes selective inattention and attention. In this case, manipulators deliberately refuse to listen or pay attention to anything that distracts them from their agendas. They always defend themselves with phrases like, 'I do not need to listen to that'.

Deviation: Controllers never answer any questions directly and always steer the discussion to another topic. If not so, the manipulator gives irrelevant or rogue answers to the direct questions asked.

Intimidation: In this case, the manipulator applies two methods of intimidation; covert intimidation and guilt trip. In underground extortion, the manipulators throw their targets onto the self-justifying side through the use of implied threats. A guilt trip is a technique where the manipulator tries to suggest to the meticulous prey that they no longer care and this makes the victim feel bad and they start doubting themselves, hence, they find themselves in a submissive position.

Use of Sarcasm: The manipulator shames the victim by using put-downs and sarcasm that makes the victim doubt themselves. Making the victim feel unworthy gives an entry for the manipulator to defer the victim. These shaming tactics may include fierce glances, unpleasant tones, rhetorical comments or questions, and subtle sarcasm. Some of the victims end up not daring to challenge the manipulator as it fosters a sagacity of meagerness to their targets. Belittling their Target: Manipulators use this technique to put their target on the self-justifying side, while at the same time, covering the belligerent aims of the persuader. The persuader then misleadingly blames their target in response to the victim's defensive mechanisms. This also involves the case where a manipulator plays the victim role by portraying themselves as victims of circumstances to gain sympathy, thereby, getting what they want. This technique aims at the caring and compassionate victims as they cannot stand seeing someone suffer, and thus, the manipulator takes that chance to get the victim's cooperation.

Feigning: Manipulator pretends that any harm caused was unintentional or they are being accused falsely. Manipulators often wear a surprised face, hence making the victim question their own sanity. Feigning also involves the case where the manipulator plays dumb and pretends they are totally unaware of what the victim is talking about. The victim starts doubting themselves while the manipulator continues to point out the main ideas they included just in case there is any doubt. This happens only if the manipulator had used cohorts in advance that helps them in backing up their stories.

Seduction: In this case, the manipulator uses praise or any form of flattery, which involves supporting the victim to gain their conviction. Manipulators can even start helping you to increase your loyalty, and it will be hard for you to suspect their ill intents. The manipulator can as well play the servant role where their actions will be justified by phrases such as, 'I am just doing my job' or 'I am in service to a certain authority figure.' In this case, the victim will give their trust and end up being manipulated.

Brandishing anger: The manipulator shows off how angry they are in order to intensify the victim's shock to get their submission. In the real sense, the manipulator is never angry, but they act like they are, especially when denied access to what they want. A manipulator can as well control their anger to avoid any confrontations or hide their intents. Manipulators often threaten the victims by saying they are going to report the cases to the police. Anger is a way of blackmailing the victim to avoid telling the truth, as it wards off any further inquiries. This makes the victim focus more on the anger of the manipulator rather than on the manipulation technique being used.

The Bandwagon effect: This is the case where the manipulator tends to comfort the victim by claiming that, whether right or wrong, many people have already done some things, and thus, the victim should do it anyway. The manipulator uses phrases like 'Many people like you...' This kind of manipulation is mainly applied to those under peer pressure conditions. Similar cases are when a manipulator tries to lure the victim into taking drugs or abusing other substances. The techniques discussed above are the tested and proven tactics that any manipulator will strive to use to get a strong control of their victims. Before a manipulator persuades their victims, there are those steps they have to follow to make sure they fully control their victim's minds.

Whatever the reasons for manipulating someone, you

should always play your cards safely. That is why you should learn how to manage and control the thoughts of people, the strategies, and steps you need to use in various situations. There are three authentic manipulating skills you can learn quickly through the steps discussed below. If you want to manipulate others in an easy way, come on! Shed a fake tear and follow the following steps.

Apply Different Persuasion and Manipulation Techniques

I. Always Start with Unreasonable Requests in order to Get More Reasonable Ones: This step is a time-tested technique for persuasion. As a manipulator, you should always start with unreasonable demands, and then wait for the victim to deny you, then follow it up with a more approachable request. It will be hard for them to reject you for the second time, as the second request will sound more appealing as compared to the first request.

II. Ask for a Rare Request before Your Real Request: This is another way of getting what you want as it entails requesting a strange thing that throws your target off guard, making them unable to deny you. Then ask for the more usual type of request, and the victim will not be able to deny it since their mind has been trained to avoid these activities.

III.   Stimulate Fear, Then Liberation: For successful persuasion, tell the person what they fear, and then relieve them of it, and with no doubt, they will be happy to grant your wish. It may sound mean, but you will get your results instantly.

IV.   Make your Target Feel Guilty: Making your target feel guilty is another step for a successful manipulation. You need to start by picking someone susceptible to feeling guilty. This should be followed by making them feel like they are bad for not granting your requests, no matter how absurd it is. The following can be the unchallenging victims who will fall into your persuasion technique:

   o   Parents - Manipulate your parents by making them feel guilty. Mention to them how you feel your life is full of sufferings since childhood because they are not granting your wishes.

- o Friends - Remind them of all the good deeds you have done for them or else tell them how they usually let you down.

- o Significant partner - Conclude your quarrels by saying 'Okay- furthermore I expected this.' This will make them feel guilty about letting you down several times.

I.   Bribe: In this step, blackmailing is not necessary to get your wishes granted. Bribe your victim with an unappealing present. You can as well offer something you would have done anyway. First, you should figure out what your targeted person wants or lacks at the moment, then try giving it to them. Secondly, do not make it sound like you are bribing, but portray yourself like someone who is willing to help your victim in return for something you want.

II. Playing the Victim: Making yourself the victim is always a great manipulation technique. You should use this step sparingly and effectively to pierce your victim's heart and get what you want. You have to act like you are a wonderful person, philanthropic, and that you are always the victim of every evil on earth. Play dumb as it makes your victim believe you are honestly perplexed by why evil things always befall you. Saying 'It is okay- I'm used to this' makes your victim feel like someone who cannot help you wall you a number of times and this tactic will make you get what you want. Finally, always be pathetic.

'It is okay- I'm used to this'

Apply Logic: This step works better for the rational-minded people. Logica; acts as the most excellent persuader, more so when you carry along with come-oriented whys and wherefores on how what you are after would benefit both of you. While presenting your case, do it calmly and rationally to avoid losing your control. If you want to manipulate a rational person, NEVER be emotional. In this step, act like your request is the only option you have, and your victim will judge the case your way.

III.   Never Break Character: When your friend, family member, or co-worker tries to manipulate you, pretend to be more upset than them. Look more hurt and tell them you are even amazed and you did not believe they could ever think that about you. This will make the victim feel guilty and sorry for you.

CHAPTER 5

IDENTIFYING MANIPULATOR TYPES

Have you ever felt a sudden lack of self-confidence or, worse, this curious and agonizing impression of not knowing how to communicate? Have you ever been deafened by doubt about your skills or qualities? Have you ever been inhabited by that feeling of inferiority that paralyzes you, chills your blood and prevents you from reacting normally? If you have ever experienced this kind of situation, it is because you have been the victim of type III manipulation and placed in the line of sight of a manipulator.

We remember that the second type of manipulator is a selfish or egocentric person who thinks only of his interests, without worrying about the consequences. But the type III manipulator, which is also called the manipulator, has a very different characteristic intention. His only goal is to destroy. Everything he undertakes is meant to kill you, to ruin what you do, or to destroy an aspect of your personality that does not suit him.

The manipulator is characterized both by his will to harm and by a formidable ability to conceal. This is why many people do not trust him or take him for another.

The manipulator does not display distinctive signs, and his perversity does not necessarily read on his face. He is a true chameleon that hides behind deceptive appearances to better destroy. He can take the appearance of a parent who is "overprotective" and who, out of selfishness, prevents his child from becoming independent. The manipulator could be a nice grandmother who, secretly, gives money to her little girl who is in rehab to, supposedly, "help her hold on". It can also be a mistress, a lover, a boss, a neighbor, a teacher, or a long-time friend. In the cozy atmosphere of the offices, it is the collaborator willing to do anything to take your place or that colleague who seeks to devalue you because your expertise is shady.

His intention is to destroy. Sometimes it may bring him something, but in this case, it's a secondary benefit because what he's essentially aiming for is the destruction of who you are, what you do, or the other of your behaviors.

Illustration

It is through these situations and testimonies that we will examine the harmful activity of a type III manipulator.

- A man wanted his son, Jean, to succeed him by also becoming a doctor at all costs. When Jean announced his desire to leave school to become a musician, his father did everything to break that dream and bring his son back to what he thought was the right path. He tried to persuade his son that he was right in seeking to destroy this vocation. "I did it for your sake, you'll thank me later," he told him then. But what he put his son through was a terrible ordeal that almost drove Jean to suicide, as he felt rejected, devalued, ridiculed, humiliated, and disavowed deep within himself.

- A husband insidiously belittles his wife, Christelle, so that she stays at home. He has nothing against her. He simply does not want her to become independent because it's not how things are done in his family, and he earns enough to make her happy. As she does not agree, he will do everything to prove (by demeaning and humiliating her) that she is unable to do without him. From his point of view, he thinks he is acting justly and in the interest of his wife. But one can easily imagine that Christelle does not see things in the same way.

- A department head, who confronts and belittles a better-performing collaborator than himself, does not necessarily feel particular hatred toward this person. He is simply trying to break the person because he feels they are a danger to him and the only way he can defend his own mediocrity is to belittle them, to diminish them, or to put him in his place so that he does not do not encroach on the department head's work. He destroys what seems to him to be a threat that could prevent him from continuing to dominate the situation. In return, the employee can talk about bullying.

The type III manipulator is a weak man who, when he feels he is in danger, tries to diminish others. He advances masked. Where a normal person tries to surpass himself to become stronger (than whatever threatens him), the manipulator has no other resource than to weaken or treacherously destroy everything that worries him.

He destroys for the sake of destruction. He is mean and does not allow others to exist on their own. He wants to control everything. We cannot impress him. It makes you feel that you are small, weak, shabby; it turns you into a "mop", it tramples you and makes you incapable of any development.

He destroys you by giving you the impression that it is for your good, but we feel very bad in his presence. We cannot win. We are not recognized for what we would like to be. He does not listen to you, and his criticism is never constructive. When he says something, it's always negative. With him, one feels humiliated, discouraged, and degraded. He is a "mental assassin" and life with him is like slavery.

Harassment and Concealed Manipulation

Type III manipulation often goes unnoticed by those who experience it. This is called harassment or hidden manipulation. A large number of victims are thus abused and destroyed without their knowledge by the deceit and duplicity of a manipulator. After two pregnancies, Chloe cannot seem to get back to the weight she was as a young girl. She explains her fight against the pounds:

"When I discover a new diet, I hasten to try it. I am sure this time will be the right one. I do what it takes, and I feel good. I have a clear mind, I am dynamic. Sometimes I even go back to playing sports. I do everything I can without effort, and I start losing weight. And then, brutally, without my understanding why, I fall back into the fog. I have no courage, I ruminate on the same black thoughts, I do not do anything, I am exhausted, and I spend my time sleeping. Then, seeing all the tasks accumulating around the apartment, I feel guilty and without realizing it, I start eating again. I call myself names while looking at my belly and my thighs in the mirror of the bathroom. Every day, I decided that, the next day, I will put myself firmly on a diet and that this time I will get there. Today, I am completely desperate because despite all my attempts, every time I get on the scale, I can see that I still gained weight."

While a hidden manipulation is hardly perceptible from

the inside, this is not the case when we observe it from the outside. This is what a friend of Chloe tells us about her weight problems:

"I have known Chloe for many years. She was always a little concerned about her weight, but it almost became an obsession from the moment she met Guillaume, her future husband. He is a charming boy, but he attaches great importance to appearances. Since Chloe gained a little weight, having had her children, he frequently comments on it. He always comments nicely, in the tone of the joke, but I think it comes a little too often. I also see that Chloe is touched, even if she pretends to laugh with the others about her 'little bulges' as she says. But I can see that deep down she is hurt when he makes fun of her in public. Moreover, in the days that follow, she regularly buys clothes that are too small, claiming that she is going to lose weight. The other night, I was at home, and he did not stop criticizing a common friend who had grown enormously. He told multiple bad jokes about his plumpness and talked about the contempt he had for people who do not know how to control their weight. When Chloe came out of the room with tears in her eyes, he suddenly changed the subject of conversation. Everyone was embarrassed, but he did not seem to notice. The worst part was that he seemed satisfied with what he had just done as if it were a good joke. I thought about Chloe, and it was really awful to see how happy he looked."

A manipulator can be extremely pleasant and user-friendly. By appearing charming, playing on someone's guild, or using a respectable or simply authoritarian position, he creates a mirage that deceives his victims and prevents them from seeing that behind his disguise of the moment, hides a purpose that is invariably destructive and harmful. Moreover, it is very difficult to blame him for the behavior because he always has an excuse to justify himself: "I am only following the instructions. I do not have the right to disobey. I only did my duty. I acted believing it was the right thing to do. It was a joke."

To be sure, we can examine (below) the two sets of symptoms that signify the presence of a manipulator. The first contains the essentials of what one feels when one is a direct victim of a manipulator and the second enumerates what one perceives as a mere observer of a hidden manipulation.

Internal Symptoms of Concealed Manipulation

These are the main internal signals that can be seen when one is a victim of type III manipulation. These symptoms are far more indicative of the presence of a manipulator than the analysis of his words or deeds:

I alternate moments of enthusiasm and discouragement. I often feel a sense of guilt or doubt.

I find it difficult to defend myself or counterattack. I feel a sudden loss of confidence in myself.

I sometimes feel that I am "drained" of my energy. I feel physical or mental discomfort in the presence of someone.

That person belittles me one way or another. It is impossible to impress or affect her.

There is always a form of ambiguity between what she does and what she says. I am not well in my head or in my body when I am around that person.

If you have at least three symptoms, there is a good chance that you have been the victim of such manipulation. When all five symptoms are reached, manipulation is certain, and you should focus on finding out for sure who the manipulator is and how he proceeds.

Generally, someone with an outside perspective can find out much more easily because they will often notice things that one who is a victim and who lives things from within misses.

Emotional Intelligence and Manipulation

The term emotional intelligence was first invented in the 1960s and has become common over the years. However, the concept behind the term has been around for decades. In simple terms, emotional intelligence is the ability of a person to recognize and understand emotions, then using this information to make decisions. Like any other skill, emotional intelligence is a skill we can cultivate, sharpen and enhance. It is important to note that although emotional intelligence is a good skill, one can use it either for good or bad.

Once a person understands the power of emotions, he/she can use it ethically or unethically. The last thing that we want is having someone manipulating our emotions, whether it is a friend, colleague, or politician. There are some ways through which a master manipulator can use emotional intelligence against you. Please note that not everyone who has the characteristics listed below and used the said skill has selfish intentions. Some people practice them with no intended harm. Nonetheless, having an increased awareness of these behaviors will empower you to deal with manipulators strategically and sharpen your intelligence quotient in the process.

1. Manipulators play on fear.

Majority of manipulators will overemphasis specific points and exaggerate facts in an effort to make you scared and have you acting as they want. The way to identify this play is by looking out for statements that imply you are not strong or courageous enough or that if you miss out on a particular thing, you are a loser.

2. Manipulators deceive

Everybody values honesty and transparency thus will avoid deceivers. Manipulators understand this concept and are very cunning when lying. They twist the facts or try to show you only the side of the story that benefits them. For instance, a work colleague can spread some unconfirmed rumor to gain an upper hand. To avoid being deceived, do not believe everything you hear. Instead, base your choices on credible sources and ask questions if the details are not clear.

3. Manipulators take advantage of your happiness

Have you noticed that you are more likely to say yes to anything when you are happy or in a good mood? When we are happy, we tend to jump on opportunities that look good even before we think things through. Master manipulators have this knowledge thus will take advantage of the moods. To manage this emotional opportunity and avoid manipulation, work to improve awareness of your emotions, both positive and negative. strive to strike a balance between logic and emotions When making decisions.

4. Manipulators take advantage of reciprocity.

Do you know that feeling you get when you owe someone a favor especially if they helped you at one point? That feeling of debt makes one vulnerable. It is hard to say no to a manipulator if you owe them something. Most of the manipulators will attempt to butter and flatter you with small favors then ask for a big one in return. As much as giving brings more joy than receiving, it is more important to know your limits. Do not be afraid to say no when you have to even if you owe someone a favor.

5. Manipulators push for a home court advantage

It is very easy to convince a person when you are in a familiar place. As such, a manipulator will push you towards meeting you in a place he/she is familiar with while you are not. Ownership gives power and comfort thus a place like home or the office will give the manipulator some authority. you will have to make requests for meeting in a neutral place where familiarity and ownership are diluted so as to disarm the manipulator.

6. The manipulator will ask a lot of questions.

Naturally, it is easy to talk about oneself. Master manipulators know this thus they take advantage to ask some probing questions. Their agendas are hidden but basically, they seek to discover your weaknesses or other information they can hold against you. Of course, it would be unfair for you to assume that everyone has wrong motives because there are a few people who genuinely seek to know you better. However, it is okay t question people, especially those who reveal nothing about themselves.

7. The manipulator will speak quickly

In order to manipulate you through your emotions, the manipulator will speak quickly and sometimes use jargon and special vocabulary. This will give them an advantage because you will not have enough time to think. Fr you to counter this form of manipulation, do not feel afraid to ask for some time to process what the person said. Also, make a point of asking the person to repeat any unclear statements. To gain some control of a conversation, repeat the points the other person makes in your own words and let them sink.

8. The display of negative emotions

Some manipulators will use voice tones to control your emotions. The most commonly used tone and body language by manipulators are negative. For instance, basketball coaches (they use manipulation for positive purposes) are masters at raising their voices and using strong body language to manipulate the emotions of the players. To avoid such manipulation, you should practice pausing. it involves taking a break from the conversation or situation and having some time to think before reacting. In fact, you may walk away for some minutes to get a grip of your own emotions.

9. Manipulators limit your time to act

Basically, every manipulator wants to win. They may do this by ensuring that you do not have enough time to think. For instance, an individual may force you to make a serious decision in an unreasonably limited amount of time. He/she will try to steer your thoughts to their advantage. You will not have enough time to weigh the consequences. To avoid a situation where you give in without thought, do not be in a rush to submit. Ensure that the demand is reasonable. Take the pause, ask for some time, and if the person does not allow you to think, walk away. You will be happier looking for whatever you need elsewhere.

10. The silent treatment.

According to Preston Ni, a manipulator will presume power in a relationship by making you wait. For instance, when a person deliberately fails to respond to your reasonable messages, calls, emails, or other inquiries, he/she makes you wait and at the same time, places uncertainty and doubt in your mind. Some manipulators use silence as leverage. To avoid being a victim of manipulation through silent treatment, give people deadlines and do not allow them to intimidate you. For instance, after attempting to communicate to a reasonable degree, let go of the mater and let the other person reach out.

Manipulators will work to increase their emotional awareness so as to have an upper hand on others. In fact, a large number of people are learning how to be emotionally intelligent. You too should seek to sharpen your emotional intelligence levels, for your own protection.

THE MOST POWERFUL MIND-POWER TOOL

Humans spend countless hours seeking new ways to work just about anything. Through endless hours of research, they pour over books and journals looking for the message that will tell them the secret to harnessing mind power. Many never realize that the most powerful mind power tool is already on board and just aching to be used. It is the human brain, the mind itself.

Every time a person practices a new habit or thinks a new thought, they make a new pathway in the brain. Every time the habit is used, or the idea is thought, the nerve pathway becomes even stronger. The human brain is wired at birth to be an efficient machine and it is ready, from birth, to make an ever increasing amount of nerve pathways and to strengthen the pathways that are used the most.

Sometimes thoughts and habits need to be changed

for the improvement of the person. When people decide that they would like to make a change in their lives, there will be a period of adjustment. This is true whether the change is mental, emotional, or physical. During this period of adjustment, there will be some level of discomfort. When a habit or a thought is already formed, it has made its own path in the brain. When a stimulus is seen or heard, the message travels along the preset nerve pathway to the spot in the brain that controls that thought or habit. In order to change a thought or a habit, it is necessary for the nerve path to be changed. Until the nerve path is changed, the old nerve path will remain in the brain. The discomfort comes from the brain trying to automatically access the old pathway and the new pathway at the same time. This is painful for the brain to do.

It is easy to become frustrated when the brain goes back to its old patterns of thought and habit. Never fall into the habit of placing blame on a lack of willpower. Willpower has nothing to do with it. It is a very difficult thing to override preset pathways in the brain. The brain is a very powerful tool. When will power fails and mistakes happen, remember to use kindness and compassion in dealing with the failure. The brain is very efficient at doing what it does. The only way to change the pathways in the brain is to keep working on new pathways that will eventually obliterate the old, undesirable ones.

The brain needs a clear understanding that changes are about to take place and new pathways are about to be laid down. Remind the brain that new habits and new thoughts will be replacing the old ones. Blaming failure on a lack of will power is a self-defeating statement. The process of making new nerve paths in the brain takes hard work and time. It will help to keep reminding oneself of the impending change. By doing this over and over, it makes the process no longer about possible character flaws. The focus is now put on the habit of thought that is being built.

Is it possible to build new nerve pathways in the brain? Yes, it is possible, and it can be done. If more proof is needed, just compare the adult brain to the baby's brain. Every current habit and thought a person has is the direct result of having spent time practicing them over and over until they created a pathway in the brain. New pathways can be created. Think of it this way: they already have. The baby's brain has no idea of anything. It has no thoughts or habits. Every nerve path currently in the brain was practiced until it became a part of the brain. Think of the baby. The baby lies around day after day and does baby things. Then one day the baby notices the shiny rattle that mommy is waving in front of its little face. The baby wants the rattle. As the baby is waving its tiny arms around, the mommy puts the rattle close enough so the baby can touch it with its wavering hand. After a few of these sessions, the baby gets the idea that if the arm is in the air it can touch the rattle. A nerve pathway is beginning to grow. So the baby decides to lift its arm to actively reach for the rattle. The baby will be unsuccessful at first because the arms will wave wildly and will not connect with the rattle. One day, the baby will actually grab the rattle, and the nerve pathway is then complete.

While this may seem like a very simple example, it is exactly how nerve pathways are created in the brain. Every action, thought, or habit has its own nerve pathway. All pathways must be created. No one was born knowing to sit in front of the television and mindlessly eat dip with chips. No one was born lamenting the excess pounds they carry in strange places. No one was born hating their body. All behaviors are learned, good and bad. And the bad ones can be replaced with good ones.

So if the ability to program negative thoughts into the brain exists, then the ability to disrupt those negative thoughts with positive thoughts also exists. The brain can be reprogrammed. It is a powerful tool, and its main function is to turn thoughts into reality. The brain is always working, so why not use the power of the brain to benefit rather than harm? Just because a particular habit or thought has been around all forever does not mean it needs to stay. Use the power of the brain to choose new habits and thoughts to focus on and replace the old, negative thought pathways in the brain.

The new thought needs to be believable; the new habit needs to be doable. It does not real good to try to stick to a habit that is impossible to accomplish or to try to believe a thought that is unbelievable. After years of seeing the reality of an obese body, it would be nearly impossible to suddenly believe that the image in the mirror is that of a skinny person. But the brain will likely accept something that mentions learning to take care of the body or learning to accept the body in order to correct its flaws. The brain will turn a belief in reality. Believing a positive thought will lead to quite a different result than the ending where only negative thoughts are present.

Be prepared to repeat and repeat some more. The primary key to being able to make a new habit stay is repeating it constantly. The more a new, desirable habit is practiced, the more the brain begins to accept it. The nerve path becomes stronger every day. With constant practice, this new nerve path will become the path the brain will prefer to use, and the old one will cease to exist.

In any case, be sure to allow enough time to effectively create a change. Accept the starting point and constantly visualize the ending point. Accept the fact that the path to the goal of a new habit or thought will not be easy or perfect. The path will almost never travel in a straight line. Sometimes people fall completely off the path, and that is okay too. Just get back up and get back on. Do not get sidetracked by the idea that this journey will be easy and carefree because it will not be. Just keep thinking of the new nerve pathway that will be created by the new thought or habit and it will eventually become a reality.

Most of the pathways in the brain are stored in the subconscious mind. This is the part of the mind that is always working without always being thought of. Think of learned skills like tying shoes, zipping a coat, and pouring milk into a glass. These were all learned behavior whose nerve pathways are firmly set in the subconscious part of the mind. This part of the brain is the bank of data for all life functions.

The communication between the conscious mind and the unconscious mind works in both directions. Whenever a person has a memory, and emotion, or an idea, it is rooted in the subconscious mind and translated to the conscious mind through mind power. The subconscious has the power to control just about anything a human does regularly.

For example, during meditation steady, deep breathing is usually practiced. The control of the breath is brought from the subconscious mind and given to the conscious mind to tell it to control the breathing. Once a pattern of deep steady breathing is begun by the conscious mind, the subconscious mind takes over and keeps the set rhythm going until it is told to stop. This is done by a conscious end to the deep breathing or an encounter with an outside stimulus like stress. The subconscious mind also processes the great wealth of information received daily and only passes along to the conscious mind those things that are necessary for the brain to remember.

When sending thoughts from the conscious mind to the subconscious mind, the brain will only send those thoughts that are attached to great emotion. The only thoughts that remain in the subconscious are those that are kept there with strong emotions. Unfortunately, the brain does not know the difference between positive emotions and negative emotions. Any strong emotion will work. Both negative emotions and positive emotions can be quite strong. Also, unfortunately, negative emotions tend to be stronger than positive emotions.

Step one in learning to use the power of the subconscious part of the mind will be to eliminate any thoughts that come with negative emotions. Also, negative mental comments will also need to cease. Fears will usually come true, specifically because they are drowning in negative emotion. This is why negative ideas need to be eliminated because they can be very harmful roadblocks on the road to harnessing brain power.

One best practice to use to get rid of negative thoughts is to counter them with positive thoughts. This will take time and practice, but it is a very powerful and useful technique. Whenever a negative thought pops in the conscious mind, immediately counter it with a positive thought that is dripping with strong emotion. The actual truth will come out somewhere in between the two thoughts.

Another way to counter negative emotions is to delete them, just like using a remote control. When a negative thought comes into the conscious mind, imagine destroying it. Imagine writing that thought on paper and burning it. Imagine pointing a remote control at the thought and pressing a huge delete button. Whatever form used to imagine deleting the thought, the important thing is to get rid of it before it can take hold in the subconscious mind.

Find something energizing and use it to reach a goal. Those things that are found to be energizing bring boundless energy to positive thoughts. It is often necessary to invent motivation, at least in the beginning, to learn to create new habits and thoughts. But with a bit of practice and a lot of positive thought, new positive habits will soon be burned into the subconscious mind and the old negative thoughts and habit will fade away.

CHAPTER 6

MASTERING YOUR EMOTIONS

Master manipulators are not at the mercy of their emotions. Instead, they have learned how to master their emotions and be in control, thus allowing themselves to think rationally while utilizing their mind instead of their feelings. If you are not in control of your emotions, you'll find yourself getting angry, sad and even frustrated in the course of your relationships. Such loss of control will be detrimental to your objective of having the upper hand. Learning how to control your emotions is a process that requires time and practice. You will not wake up one day and be a happy, confident person that never gets angry or sad. It is not an overnight process.

To control your emotions, you will need a period of time to go through the motions of recognizing your emotions and reigning in on them. Train yourself not to react immediately and irrationally to every emotion that presents itself in your life. Instead, step back and process this emotion by identifying what triggered it and what solutions you can apply to alleviate this trigger. For instance, if you get angry whenever someone makes a particular comment about you, you might want to go back and understand why this comment upsets you so much. Once you work on the root cause, you can thereafter start the process of being unbothered by such a comment.

In certain other instances, you might want to think of your relationships as business transactions where nothing should be taken personally. Detaching yourself from people will mean having fewer emotions to deal with as you will no longer be affected by their opinions about you. Instead, you will look at them from a benefits point of view where you take what you need and then go on your merry way. If you come across as the emotionally stable guy who can control himself in any situation, people will begin to trust you a little bit better. This is a handy advantage to have over others when you are trying to manipulate them subtly.

Timing and opportunity

No matter how good of a manipulator you are, you will never be successful if you do not get your timing right. There are instances where your tactics will not work, and not because they are not good enough, but because your timing is off. It is important to know when your target is more susceptible to manipulation, and when they just do not have the time to deal with you. Identifying the right opportunities will guarantee you far more success as opposed to going about the process haphazardly. Why do you think retail stores have sales at particular times of the month? They know that at this time their customers have the money and are ready to be manipulated aka indulge in some shopping.

Choosing a time that is most convenient for your target will yield better results for you. Consider this: you are trying to relax on the beach when this salesperson comes to you trying to sell you something. What are you likely to say? If you are a normal human being that likes their alone time and does not take well to vacation intruders, you will send the salesperson on their merry way--complete with a cuss word or two. What this salesperson does not know (besides proper etiquette) is that they chose the very worst of times--a time that was not convenient for you. As such, you will be looking to get rid of them and whatever they have to sell as swiftly as possible.

There are times in the day when you are likely to hear "yes" more often than "no". It is important to identify these times and then work them to your advantage. Sometimes, the issue of convenience is ignored, and it becomes a matter of vulnerability. A person who is tired is less likely to put up a fight. A boss who is rushing to catch a flight might be more inclined to say yes to your question so that they can be done with you and head for the airport. When it comes to timing and opportunity, you must balance the facts with your own assessment of every individual situation.

Physical contact

Physical contact is one of the most powerful tools at the disposal of a human being. A hug from a loved one, a pat on the back by a family member and even a cuddle with someone you are close to can do wonders for the human spirit. Soft, gentle, safe touch is healing to the human soul. It reassures the other party and creates an emotional connection. The firm touch of a masseuse kneading away at your tense muscles if rejuvenating. An innocent brush of the fingers with a stranger or a date might be all you need to know whether they are the one or not. When touched correctly, your body's stress hormone (cortisol) levels reduce while the happy hormones go up. You might not be aware of these fluctuating hormones, but you will instantly feel happier and lighter when properly touched. It is no wonder that merely hugging a loved one can take away all your worries instantly. In this state of happiness--and less cortisol cruising around their body--a person is not in flight or fight mode anymore and will likely comply with your requests.

If you are trying to make someone feel safe and secure around you, to the point where they can trust you, make use of the power of touch. There are different types of touch. The type of touch you choose will depend on the type of relationship you have with the other party. Seeing that touch is so powerful, it is important to acknowledge the double-edged sword that it is. Your touch can either make someone feel particularly comfortable around you or the exact opposite. The last thing you want to do is creep someone out when all you are trying to do is get them to agree to work your shift for you.

Here's the proper way to use physical contact to your benefit:

Watch their body language for signs that your touch will be well-received. Such signs include an upright posture coupled with a happy or neutral facial expression. If the person has a negative facial expression and seems to be hunched over, walk away. Such a person will not take kindly to your touching.

There is a safe zone for touching someone that is not well-known to you. This safe zone is the region between the elbow and shoulder. Any touch within this area is likely to be well-received, especially if you already determined that their body language is open to it. Consider touching this safe zone while shaking the other person's hand, as it would be awkward to just walk up to someone and touch their upper arm.

To properly touch someone, it must seem as if your action was entirely unplanned and spontaneous. The last thing you need is someone noticing that you planned to touch them because this would come across as creepy and awkward. Make your technique so swift and smooth that your touch comes and goes like a whisper in the wind. Do not touch and linger; touch and let go, in the most seamless execution that you can master. This is the difference between being a charming and affectionate guy and being the creep that everyone avoids.

Be confident when touching a person. People can tell if you are insecure about what you are doing, and this not only puts them off, but it also makes them incredibly uncomfortable. If you want to touch someone in order to make them compliant with your request, go for it without hesitation. Make it seem as if you have been touching people all your life. Remember that lack of confidence can show itself in your body language, so make sure you have taken care of this as well. Stand tall and exude confidence--then touch your target.

Smile as you touch your target. By touching this person, you are showing yourself to be open to them and willing them to be open to you. The rest of your body must communicate this. Do not touch someone while wearing a sour face, as this will come off as aggressive. Smiling makes you look more warm, welcoming and open, and your target will think that you are just a happy person who likes to be affectionate.

Fear and Manipulation

Why is fear such an effective tool in manipulation? Why do companies like to threaten you into compliance by asking you to buy something before stocks run out when they know full well that they have an entire warehouse of products? Why do manipulators like to instill fear in their victims? Fear is a negative emotion whose presence in the body inhibits rational decision making. Here's why:

When you are scared, there are only two thoughts on your mind: fight or flight. Nothing else. You really do not have the mind to start engaging in critical thinking or anything of the sort. Being scared or anxious sends your body into survival mode, and when you are in survival mode, you will choose one of two options that make the most sense to you. The neuroscience behind this is critical to understanding what makes fear such a favorite tool for manipulators. When your entire bodily systems are in that flight-or-flight response mode, your critical thinking circuitry is bypassed. In short, your brain does not have the intention to start processing the tiny details at the moment. So, instead of utilizing the more analytical neocortex to think, you rely on the primitive limbic system. Later on, when you are in a more relaxed state, your critical thinking capability is activated, and you start to wonder why you made that particular decision when in fact there were other options to explore.

At all times, be careful of anyone who cries wolf. They might be trying to distract you from the other options that are available to be explored in your decision-making. At the same time, you must take advantage of the opportunity presented by fear to influence other people. There are various ways of taking advantage of fear in situations. For a start, you can exaggerate a situation and make it seem far worse than it is. Let's say you are a manager and you catch this one employee skipping work without official leave. It's a slow day anyway, and there's not much work to be done--but they know they should not be skipping work, and you intend to take full advantage of this situation.

What to do? For a start, you need to make this seem like the biggest deal of the century. How dare they hide from work and expect to receive a paycheck at the end of the month? Do they know what would happen if this got to the other bosses? You might even want to mention that they have put you in a really awkward position by engaging in such a foolish act. Now that you have got your employee shaking in their boots (assuming that they really need the job and the paycheck) ask them whether they would be willing to work the weekend shift to make up for this lost time, in exchange for a slap on the wrist. The employee will most likely say yes. They have not had time to even come up with a good lie because their minds are in flight or fight mode. You'll then go on about your day happily knowing full well that you do not have to work the weekend shift and can instead spend the day doing what you truly enjoy.

Aside from exaggerating the truth, you can instill fear by spreading blatant lies. This approach has worked since time immemorial and continues to be effective to date. Using the same example of a manager, let's assume you have noticed that the employees are slacking in their duties, including coming in late for work and generally being lazy. You have tried all means to motivate them, and nothing seems to be working. What can you do? Consider this: find the one employee with the loosest mouth and let it slip that there will be an impromptu performance review by management sometime soon. This loose-lipped employee will do the legwork for you and ensure that the entire rumor mill knows what's about to happen. You will begin to notice that your employees are working harder and coming to work earlier because they are fearful of the consequences of facing management.

Fear in manipulation works best where the party that is being manipulated stands to lose or miss out on something. You must determine that whatever carrot you are dangling in front of your victim is worth their attention. Otherwise there will be no interest and consequently, no success in your manipulation efforts. If you know what makes someone tick, you will always know what buttons to push to make them fearful.

Raising Your Emotional Cleverness

Emotional intelligence is definitely something you have to work on throughout life. There are professions, or lifestyles, where high emotional intelligence might not be that necessary, however, the majority of us could do with better people skills, both in and outside function.

There are many ways of enhancing or developing your emotional intelligence. However, whichever method you choose to use, your time and efforts should concentrate on the seven simple routines which will help increase your EQ and indirectly make it easier to reach your goals, whatever they might be.

7 ways to increase your emotional intelligence:

Develop self-awareness

Self-awareness is about self-knowledge, about getting mindful of what is happening in your life, and about having an idea how you see your daily life or career developing. To be self-aware you need a certain degree of maturity and at least a vague idea of what you'd like to do with your existence. When you know what you want, it becomes easier to find a method of getting it. If you don't, you are left drifting aimlessly, with neither a goal nor a plan.

So, how can you develop self-awareness? Begin by increasing your sensitivity to your very own gut and emotions emotions, as they are generally the most trusted close friends you'll ever have. Make an effort to set aside a while for self-reflection, and think about your behavior, thoughts, emotions, frustrations, goals, etc.

Those who are used to self-analysis will find this easy probably, but if you're not used to this type or sort of thinking, this may be hard, even unsettling. In that full case, start by setting aside 30 minutes each night, once you're finished with the work for the day and may relax a bit, and think about the day or week behind you. If you had a difficult day/week particularly, ask yourself everything you can find out from the experience.

The purpose of this exercise is to truly get you used to considering how you feel and why.

Or, you may start journaling, and this is not about keeping a diary and covering your day-to-day thoughts and activities. Journaling is about recording any unusual or frustrating experiences, thoughts or emotions you might have had. Some things are not easy to go over with others, and anyway, not really everything is for posting, so why not get it off your chest by authoring it. The great thing about journaling is normally that to write something down, you need to believe about what to write, in fact it is often this technique of thinking about a problem that helps you see what's at the root of it. Therefore, if feeling upset, angry or disappointed, write it out and move on.

Understand your emotions and what triggers them

To comprehend your emotions you have to be willing to experience them. It's sad just how many people are afraid of their own emotions, especially negative ones, eg sadness, anger, bitterness, etc and the moment they feel these feelings taking over, they perform something that may interrupt their train of thought, eg they could active themselves with something in order to distract themselves from these unpleasant emotions.

In the event that you recognize yourself in this, you should know that all you will achieve this way is postpone (perhaps indefinitely) facing your own demons and dealing with whatever it is that's troubling you. Feelings need to be experienced and dealt with, not buried.

Intelligent folks are not scared of their emotions emotionally. Whatever it really is they feel, they keep at it for so long as it requires for the emotion to end up being identified. There is a reason you feel how you do, and instead of ignoring them, you should try to "decipher" your emotions because they are trying to let you know something.

To become proficient at understanding others, you first have to be able to understand yourself. So, even the emotions you don't actually want to feel should be addressed, processed, and let go.

Listen without judging

Good listeners are uncommon, mainly because this involves a whole lot of empathy, willingness to give up your time and effort for others, and mental energy to be present when you are listening.

The primary trait of a good listener is to pay attention with empathy, and which means without judging. This is not easy always, and may in a few full cases be difficult, so if you understand you are biased towards someone, it's perhaps better not to talk to them in the event that you know you have already made up your mind about how you are feeling about what they are going to say.

So, to become a great listener you should attempt to be present during the conversation, and stay focused. This can be hard, as some social people don't stop talking, or have a problem stating what they mean so you may be looking at a few hours. However, if you are not interested in this person really, or you are in a rush, or are not feeling well, try to postpone the conversation for another time. The tell-tale indications of disinterest or boredom, eg glancing at your watch, or checking your cell emails or phone, can be extremely insulting and discouraging for the person you are having a conversation with.

Emotionally intelligent people show interest in others by encouraging them to speak even more (even if indeed they don't agree with what they are saying), and by creating a host where it's safe to start and say everything you really mean.

So, the next time you speak to a person who requirements your opinion, advice or simply a shoulder to cry on, try to be patient (some people have a long time to come to the point), focused (reserve this time limited to them and switch off your phone), and non-judgemental (provide them with the benefit of a doubt). By not becoming and judging open-minded, you might not only help the person by giving them an opportunity to obtain something off their upper body, nevertheless, you may also gain insight into what's going on in your team, or a family.

Also, focus on body language, both yours' and theirs', eg the modulation of voice, facial expression, body posture, etc. To a casual observer, these would be clear symptoms how you both feel about the conversation.

Active listening takes a complete lot of practice, but it is among those skills that you can practice every full day, of where you are regardless, and what it really is you are listening to.

Mind-Body Connection

This is about listening to the body and understanding what it's trying to tell you. According to the mind-body connection doctrine, irritation in a part of your body is definitely a sure indication something is not right. For instance, lower back discomfort is linked to financial problems, upper back discomfort to being overwhelmed with life, a knot in the tummy with nervousness or fear, etc.

Understanding how to notice these signals and interpret them, can help you save considerable time and difficulty with regards to understanding why you feel a certain way.

But, what frequently happens is that while your body is informing you that you are anxious, anxious, angry, or harm, you ignore these symptoms simply, hoping they would eventually go away.

Unfortunately, Western culture pays an excessive amount of importance to feeling happy and high at all times, so folks are not encouraged to deal with their negative feelings, but are advised to ignore them, eg by repeating positive affirmations, or repair them, by taking something that will make them experience better. Do you really believe that if you ignore your adverse feelings, do it again a mantra or take something to make you feel high, you will eventually become happy, confident, and fearless???

Sometimes, when you're overwhelmed with emotions, it may be OK to calm yourself straight down, in unhealthy ways even, until you may clearly think. But, this only gives temporary respite and is not a solution to your problem.

Emotional intelligence will help you get to underneath of your emotions by showing you how exactly to work out what the triggers are, and how exactly to interpret and release these emotions in the least harmful way.

Engage

How involved are you with your community? Do you volunteer? Is there someone you are helping with by moral support frequently, financially or otherwise? Are you there for others if they need you even though you know it'll ruin your weekend which you had planned to invest with your family?

Empathy is the primary trait of intelligent people emotionally, and it could easily be developed by anyone if they follow a couple of simple tips on how to develop or improve these abilities. But, the simplest way to develop empathy can be through practicing it. Put simply, whenever you engage with others, you are doing what emotionally smart people do: you listen, you try to understand, you listen in.

Nevertheless, many people fake empathy due to the fact they'd like to be observed simply because emotionally intelligent. They say the right matter, are politically correct always, appear to be filled with deep empathy, listen thoroughly, offer help, etc. However, if caught off-safeguard or if for a few good reason not feeling in the feeling for putting up an act, their true character quickly comes out. Today, to advance professionally, if you see yourself as a head especially, you have to prove that you have high psychological intelligence, so those that fake it do that for self-promotion usually.

The easiest way to improve your empathy is to start taking interest in others, eg how they live, what's troubling them, how they cope, etc. Improve your listening skills and try to possess at least one deep conversation per month. By engaging with others, you automatically increase your emotional intelligence.

Develop self-management

Self-management is about controlling your emotions, not in the feeling that you suppress them or ignore them, but figure out how to deal with them, and only release them after you have processed and understood them. Self-management is also about being accurate to yourself. Some of the real ways you can improve your self-administration are through developing your integrity, eg:

- Practice what you preach

- Be prepared to speak up, even though you risk being made fun of

- Don't make promises you are unlikely to keep

- Continually be polite and respectful with co-workers, it doesn't matter how close you might be

- Be self-disciplined, especially if you anticipate that of others

Learn to cope with criticism

Negative feedback is usually often undeserved and a result of the person presenting it is not fully aware of your performance, or using the opportunity to sabotage your self-confidence perhaps, or undermine your job openly.

However, if truth be told, atlanta divorce attorneys negative feedback there is usually a grain of truth. Although there might have been very good reasons why you underperformed or experienced a score of people complain about you, the truth is you failed. However, when you come to a stage when you're able to accept negative opinions, or open criticism, without taking it you demonstrate which you have both self-confidence and psychological intelligence personally.

So, how to become more open to negative feedback? Of all first, not all criticism is important equally, nor should you react to it in the same way. A colleague's remark about your brand-new hairstyle is actually a sign she's making fun of you, nonetheless it may be a subtle suggestion that the design doesn't suit you.

Besides, in the event that you receive less than satisfactory feedback on your own performance repeatedly, or behavior, instead of sulking or throwing a tantrum, try to look in yourself through other people's eye. Imagine if you ARE lazy actually, or short-tempered, or unreliable?

The key thing is to consider why you are feeling bad about the feedback. Is it because it's really undeserved and due to the person giving it devoid of a complete picture, or are you angry with yourself for not having masked your underperformance better? Or simply jealous others do better?

Admitting you were wrong isn't easy, but surviving in denial is even worse. So, than experience upset about the opinions rather, try to find out something from it. Especially if it's not the very first time the same thing have been brought to your attention.

But, regardless of how you feel, be aware that negative feedback, if given without malice, can perform more for your personal development, than can false praise.

Besides, there is something noble about admitting you had been wrong. It could not be a pleasant thing to do, but it teaches you are mature more than enough to take both the credit for your successes and blame for your errors. This may encourage others to do the same.

The effects of emotional manipulation

Manipulation is a mechanism that the affective manipulator uses to assert itself due to a lack of self-confidence even though it seems resolved and decided.

He needs to have many individuals around him to continually confront and humiliate them to feel successful. The needs of those around him are not taken into consideration.

He is a true self-centered whose only goal is to admit that he is the best, denigrating the other. To humiliate one's victim has the aim of affirming her presumed superiority through direct criticism, irony, and indifference.

The manipulation produces devastating effects on those who suffer it, generates feelings of guilt, aggression, anxiety, fear, and sadness.

On the physical plane, migraines, digestive disorders, lack of appetite or bulimia, knots in the stomach or throat and sleep disorders emerge.

If exposure to a manipulator is prolonged, these symptoms can turn into disease, which can also be followed by depression that can sometimes culminate in suicide.

Emotional counter-manipulation the fogging technique

No manipulator will ever admit to being the cause of these disorders, indeed. He will advise those affected to seek treatment without ever questioning themselves. The only way to defend yourself from an affectionate vampire's attacks is to not approach or manipulate them.

According to the therapist I. Nazare Aga, the manipulation of the "fog" consists of using vague and imprecise communication, not engaging in the verbal exchange.

The purpose of a superficial communication is to respond as if you were indifferent to the contents expressed by the manipulator, which consequently will no longer feel important. Communicating without aggression and vehemence will make the manipulator understand that the interlocutor is putting in place a passive resistance and this will lead him to spontaneously move away from the victim.

The most common verbal methods to counter manipulate are

- Not telling the details of one's own life, using a vague communication.

- Not answering uncleared questions.

- Not believing those who give compliments without knowing you.

- Communicating clearly when you don't agree.

- To express oneself firmly.

- Recognize the responsibility for one's actions and delimit it rationally. Whoever becomes the prey of an affective vampire does not recognize the danger and is in need of receiving the approval of others for their own choices.

Raising your Self-Esteem Levels

All of the aforementioned reasons a manipulator chooses a victim are related to self-esteem levels of the victim. It's very easy to fall into a pattern of nitpicking at everything we do wrong. I'll give you a personal example.

A few months ago I missed a deadline with a client at work and I felt terrible about it. Meanwhile, I had been doing awesome with other projects and excelling in areas that I never thought I would excel in, but that one missed deadline seemed to drag me down. The rest of my projects suffered and I ended up missing more due to my lack of motivation and ultimately, the low self-esteem I was beginning to suffer from due to stress. It doesn't take much to drag a person down in today's rough and tumble economy where we're constantly competing for jobs, love, and respect.

That's why it's extremely important to follow some of these steps to keep your self-esteem boosted that you are in a better position to defend yourself against the ruthless manipulators out there who want to drag you down.

Thirteen Ways to Boost Your Self-Esteem

These thirteen ways will help you boost your self-esteem levels so that you can handle the people who are attempting to manipulate you. If these do not help, I strongly suggest you see a therapist to get some more tips and discuss why you're feeling so low about yourself.

Start with Something Small

You're not going to change your outlook in just one day, so start with something small and easily obtained in order to give yourself a gentle boost in the right direction. It's like trying to clean an entire house that is stacked full of junk. You have to start somewhere, so start in the hall closet and celebrate your success. Then move on to the kitchen and keep going to each different room. Before you know it, the entire house is clean and your self-esteem has elevated.

Use Visualization and Make it Compelling

Your imagination is a very powerful tool and you should utilize it is often as possible when it comes to your self-esteem. When you imagine an outcome, make it positive and reinforcing, not doom and gloom. Take ten minutes every morning and find a quiet place in your home. Visualize how you want to be as a confident person and then write down all of those attributes you saw in yourself. By doing this, you are training your subconscious to behave the way you want to be.

Don't Underestimate the Power of Socializing

Find people who will support you no matter what and hang out with them more often. They will give you an opportunity to practice your interpersonal skills and help you see that there are other people out there who care about you. You don't need to rely on one person for your happiness.

Do Something that Frightens You

If you're afraid of going out to parties, go out to one alone and experience it to its fullest. Don't rely on someone else to hold your hand through the situation, and if you need to, practice some breathing exercises to get through it.

Do Something You're Good At

It doesn't matter what it is. It could be painting model

airplanes or even crunching numbers for a budget. Do something that you know you're good at and that you will excel at so that you feel accomplished. This will boost your confidence sky high.

Have Goals

Without goals, you have no idea where you're going in life and whether or not you've accomplished something. You should always have something you're working toward and always reward yourself when you're finished with a goal. It doesn't matter if your first goal is to clean the bathroom, do it and reward yourself for taking the actionable steps to clean the bathroom. By accomplishing things and feeling good about them, we're boosting our self-esteem levels.

Helps Others Feel Good

Give others compliments when they're feeling low or teach them something they've always wanted to learn. By helping others, you're helping yourself feel wanted and productive. Just be sure that the people you're helping are not manipulators. Do not allow them to have control over the situation and always be aware of those who are trying to take advantage of you.

Get Clarity

You need to have a clear idea of where you are at your lowest on a self-esteem scale and which category you need to work on first. There are three main categories: health, relationships, and finances. Rate yourself on a scale of one to ten through those categories, and work on the one that is at its lowest point. By doing this, you will boost your self-esteem in all the other areas, too.

Have a Plan

Treat your life as if you're baking a cake. You need actionable steps in order to accomplish your goals, so make a list of small goals beneath your large one and then make a list of tasks underneath those goals. Take everything a step at a time so you don't become overwhelmed and quit prematurely. This will only hurt your self-esteem, so you have to be ready with a plan when you have a goal.

Become Motivated

It can be as simple as setting rewards for each milestone you complete underneath a goal, or it could be reading an inspirational book. We find inspiration and strengthen in others' ability to overcome hardships, so find something that really makes you want to get started.

Get External Compliments

It may seem awkward and a little odd, but go to a family member or a friend and ask them to be honest with you about your strengths and what they love about you. Sometimes we need to hear someone else tell us what we're good at, but don't rely on this too much. Take those strengths and expand on them with the knowledge you have about yourself.

Use Affirmations

Affirmations have to be used in the correct way in order to be productive and helpful. You cannot be sitting on your couch and tell yourself that you are highly motivated and productive. Instead, ask yourself why you're sitting on the couch and is this your best self? Is this what you want to be doing right now in order to be ideal? Your affirmations must be the truth, and not something that you want to be true. You have to be honest with yourself and take the first step toward doing something of value.

It would be empty words with no meaning if you sat down in front of a mirror and told yourself you were beautiful every morning without believing those words. You have to dig deep and find the belief that you are beautiful inside and mentally repeat it in order to make it stick.

Stop Comparing Yourself to Others

All too often we're stuck in this vicious cycle of comparing ourselves to others. We need to know what the latest fashion models are wearing so that we can emulate them. If our coworker has something that's better than what we have, well then, we must not be worthy of love or companionship. Stop looking to others for how you should feel about yourself. Just accept that you have to move at your own pace and travel your own path to becoming the person you want to be.

The Art of Subliminal Messages

Subliminal and dark psychology

Subliminal impact and subliminal informing are terms used to depict when messages are disguised out of sight of clamor (for example music, radio communicates, business jingles, and so forth.) or potentially pictures to embed specific data in your subliminal musings.

Reason

The thought is that your conscious personality can't recognize these messages, and in this manner, the subliminal mandate is ingested unchallenged into your intuitive where it can impact your contemplations and conduct. If you can deliberately recognize the message, at that point, it wasn't subliminal

One of the most well-known instances of subliminal informing are messages played during rest. ... In any case, in spite of it being made up, individuals weren't excessively content with the idea of this subliminal advertising.

Subliminal messages are boosts that lie beneath the edge of conscious mindfulness. ... Any change you need to make that can't be framed by mindfulness MUST be made on the intuitive personality level. The subliminal Affirmations in the sound is short explanations that rehash again and again.

A concealed message is data that isn't quickly recognizable, and that must be found or revealed and deciphered before it very well may be known. Shrouded messages incorporate in reverse sound messages, concealed visual messages, and symbolic or secretive codes, for example, a crossword or figure.

Laws. The United States does not have a particular government or state law tending to the utilization of subliminal messages in promoting. Instead, it is the nation's publicizing and broadcasting administrative organizations that manage the point and its effect on general society.

Anything a body can normally do you can summon with entrancing or subliminal messages. If it's outside of the body's capacity, you can't. So you can move digestion. However, you can't develop wings.

Dark psychology

Dark Psychology is the workmanship and study of manipulation and mind control. While Psychology is the investigation of human behavior and is integral to the considerations, activities, and connections, the term Dark Psychology is the marvel by which people use tactics of inspiration, persuasion, manipulation, and intimidation to get what they need.

While dealing with the doctorate and examining irregular psychology, a term called "The Dark Triad" that alludes to what numerous criminologist and analyst pinpoint as a simple indicator of criminal behavior, just as problematic, broken connections. The Dark Triad incorporates the qualities of ...

Dark Psychology Triad

Narcissism – Egotism, pomposity, and absence of compassion.

Machiavellianism – Uses manipulation to trick and endeavor people and has no sense of ethical quality.

Psychopathy – Often enchanting and well disposed at this point is described by impulsivity, selfishness, absence of compassion, and callousness.

None of us need to be a casualty of manipulation, yet it happens frequently. We may not be liable to someone specifically in the Dark Triad, however ordinary, everyday people like you face dark psychology tactics once a day.

These tactics are frequently found in plugs, web promotions, deals systems, and even the supervisor's behaviors. If you have children (particularly young people), you will, without a doubt, experience these tactics as your youngsters explore different avenues regarding behaviors to get what they need and look for independence. Clandestine manipulation and dark persuasion are regularly used by people you trust and love. Here is a portion of the tactics periodically used by typical, everyday people.

Love Flooding – Compliments, fondness or adulating someone to make a solicitation

Lying – Exaggeration, falsehoods, fractional realities, false stories

Love Denial – Withhold consideration and warmth.

Withdrawal – Avoiding the individual or quiet treatment

Decision confinement – Giving specific decision alternatives that divert from the decision you don't need someone to make

Turn around Psychology – Tell an individual a specific something or to accomplish something to inspire them to do the contrary, which is genuinely what you want.

Semantic Manipulation – Using words that are expected to have a typical or common definition.

Who uses Dark Psychology and manipulation tactics? Here's a rundown of people who appear to use these tactics the most.

Narcissists – People who are genuinely narcissistic (meeting clinical diagnosis) have an expanded sense of self-worth. They need others to approve their conviction of being predominant. They have dreams of being venerated and revered. They use dark psychology tactics, manipulation, and untrustworthy persuasion to keep up.

Sociopaths – People who are genuinely sociopathic

(meeting clinical diagnosis), are regularly beguiling, smart, yet incautious. Because of an absence of emotionality and capacity to feel regret, they use dark tactics to assemble a shallow relationship and after that exploit people.

Lawyers – Some lawyers center so eagerly around winning their case that they resort to utilizing dark persuasion tactics to get the result they need.

Lawmakers – Some government officials use dark psychological tactics and dark persuasion tactics to persuade people they are correct and to get cast a ballot.

Sales reps – Many salespeople become so focused on accomplishing a deal that they use dark tactics to inspire and convince someone to purchase their item.

Leaders – Some leaders use dark tactics to get consistency, more noteworthy exertion, or higher execution from their subordinates.

Open Speakers – Some speakers use dark tactics to increase the enthusiastic condition of the group of spectators, realizing it prompts selling more items at the back of the room.

Selfish People – This can be any individual who has a motivation of self before others. They will use tactics to address their very own issues first, even at someone else's cost. They don't mind win-lose results.

People attempt a wide range of things to recover their ex yet some of the time they come up short. Dark psychological strategies may assist you with getting your ex back powerless to resist you in a short time. There are a few procedures to recover your ex; however, they ought to be connected methodically to get excellent outcomes.

We as a whole, on occasion face some agitated minutes and the most horrifying thing in life is when your cherished one leaves you. There are various approaches to recover your ex throughout time; however, some tolerance is vital. Do whatever it takes not to surrender all expectations regarding sparing your relationship and give your total endeavors to recover your ex.

The Dark Psychological Strategies

Claim to their sense of interest. Interest is an incredible driving variable in the majority of the makeups. People will go along to what you wish to fulfill their curiosity.

Stir their self-interest. Self-interest is a unique spark in each one of us. Many will go to unimaginable lengths to gratify their selfishness.

Try not to attempt to surge indiscriminately to recover your ex. Set up an idiot-proof intend to approach your ex. The precise approach will assist you with getting accomplish your closures. As a matter of first importance be arranged sincerely and rationally and afterward proceed considering the arrangement you have. Adopt time to strategy your ex as hustling won't take care of your problem.

Be sure on the means you take to recover your ex. Energy the correct way will assist you with getting out from the condition you are in. Approach your ex in an efficient mode with your readied arrangement. Taking assistance from your companions will likewise assist you with solving your problem as they can consistently and bolster you.

Attempt to talk about the things with your ex transparently and furthermore do whatever it takes not to conceal items. Point to point talk will assist you in solving the problem. Attempt to gift the things which your ex loves in your meeting as it will please and the odds of taking care of the problem will likewise increment. Be agreeable when you are chatting with your ex. In this way, these are a portion of the things to remember as you continue to your subsequent stage.

CONCLUSION

Throughout this book, we have discussed all of the things that are important to remember to avoid being manipulated, and to include positive persuasion in the way that you interact with others. It isn't something that is going to be achieved overnight, but with more and more practice, you can remember that you have what it takes to get the things that you desire most.

The biggest mistake that some will make after learning of these methods is to use them to only their advantage and take from others rather than spreading the happiness and satisfaction received through influence. It is a lot easier to negatively manipulate someone than to positively persuade them. Sometimes, persuasion means building trust.

Manipulation can simply mean instilling fear. While manipulation might be easier, it is going to cause a lot more difficult things in the end that you will have to clean up afterwards!

Remember that this process starts with really

understanding someone's personality. There are common types of manipulators out there and you might be able to sense this personality trait in another person right away. Similarly, you will also recognize that there are hidden qualities that won't always emerge at first.

Remember to recognize that not all manipulative behaviors presented by an individual indicates that she is a malicious person. Having manipulative parents or long-term partners can rub off on our behavior, so we might sometimes say and do things that aren't meant to be manipulative but can come off that way. Always look at intention when determining if someone is really being manipulative or not.

Also, don't forget that body language can play a huge role in how someone will be perceived. You can start to see persuasive body language in others more often than you did before as soon as you become aware of what this kind of body language looks like. Ensure you are aware of your own body language as well so as not to be manipulated by others.

At the end of the day, manipulation is generally a way

for a person to get the things that they desire most. We all have basic human needs and instincts that drive our behavior. If we are not careful with how we go about getting these things, we can hurt others. The more equipped we are with the skills needed for positive influence, the easier it will be to achieve our deepest desires in a healthy way that benefits many.

To continue to grow your level of influence, remember that it starts with small moments of persuasion. Don't tell people what to do, encourage them from personal experience and stories learned from others. Don't try and trick someone into doing the things they don't want to do. Be honest with reward and consequence so that they can properly make the decision for themselves.

Always ensure that you are reflecting on your own behavior to make sure that you aren't going about things in the wrong way. With becoming influential, there is a certain level of confidence that comes along as well. If you are not careful, that confidence will drive you too far ahead of others, and you can get lost in what you perceive to be best for everyone. The better you can reflect and ensure you have the right intention, the easier it will be for others to be legitimately inspired by you.

While it might be hard to do the right thing in times where what is easiest will also benefit you the most, remember to be empathetic towards others. Though it might be challenging, you will still ultimately get the things you desire most when you are doing so in a fair and rewarding way.

www.ingramcontent.com/pod-product-compliance
Lightning Source LLC
Chambersburg PA
CBHW050729030426
42336CB00012B/1488